HABITS of the HEART

How to Develop Winning Character

ELMER TOWNS

DESTINY IMAGE® PUBLISHERS, INC.
P.O. Box 310, Shippensburg, PA 17257-0310
"Promoting Inspired Lives."

This book and all other Destiny Image and Destiny Image Fiction books are available at Christian bookstores and distributors worldwide.

For more information on foreign distributors, call 717-532-3040.

Reach us on the Internet: www.destinyimage.com.

ISBN 13 TP: 978-0-7684-7600-2

ISBN 13 eBook: 978-0-7684-7601-9

For Worldwide Distribution.

1 2 3 4 5 6 7 8 / 27 26 25 24 23

TABLE OF CONTENTS

PART THREE

PART FOUR

PART ONE

HABITS OF THE HEART

Chapter 1:

HOW TO FORMULATE CHARACTER

A T the very heart of what it means to be a Christian is faith. Without faith it is impossible to please God (Heb. 11:6). One of the first descriptions of Christians in the early church was the expression "believers" (Acts 5:14). But the kind of faith that impresses God and characterized those early Christians is a faith that impacts the way we live. "For as the body without the spirit is dead, so faith without works is dead also" (James 2:26). Biblical faith shows up in the way we live our life.

The absence of godly character in Christians has a tendency to weaken the impact of Christianity on society. Both in the fall of prominent televangelists and the less prominent scandals associated with the lives of lay Christians in our church, non-Christians have been given ample opportunity to legitimately question the value of our faith. Why should they adopt a faith which doesn't seem to work for those who already adhere to it?

But the good news is that through the development of godly character we can once again restore credibility to the message we preach. When people see the Gospel making a difference in our life, they will be attracted to the Gospel which is able to make that difference. Just as the bright petals of a flower draw a bee to the sweet nectar inside, so a consistent Christian character will draw others to the Christ who indwells us and enables us to live the Christian life.

A correlation exists between what we believe (our creed or the content of our faith), the process by which we believe (the foundation of our faith), how we live (our actions and habits), and who we are (our character). This chapter examines the process by which we form character. It tells us how to develop the moral character that will attract others to Christ rather than create a barrier between them and the Gospel.

In his second epistle, the apostle Peter summarizes the process of developing that kind of character. I have paraphrased this key passage to help us understand the process more completely. "God has given us powerful yet precious promises in Scripture that will break our old lust and change us to become followers of Christ.

To change, add faith to your knowledge of Scripture, then add virtue (estimation or expectation), next add the attitude of Self-control (temperance), also add patient actions, and finally, the results will make you live like God, become kind, and love others. If these qualities increase in you, they will keep you from being ineffective and unproductive" (2 Peter 1:4-8, ELT).

Let's take a closer look at each step in the process of developing character. This belief system cycle is the basis for character development in our life.

WHEN YOU CHANGE YOUR THINKING, YOU CHANGE YOUR BELIEFS

What you believe does make a difference. In the Scriptures, belief is not just a mental decision. It is a commitment to a life of discipleship. Those who were first called believers were soon called disciples as the watching world saw how their faith changed the way they lived their life (Acts 6:1).

Belief may be defined as the conviction that something is true. The Scriptures use various words to describe belief which when examined together outline the normal steps to developing Biblical belief. First, the word "hope" describes the desires we may have. On the basis of this hope, we make plans which reflect what we anticipate. As we are persuaded in our faith, we express our confidence. The fullest expression of our confidence is the statement "I know." When we come to that point in the growth of our faith, we have moved into the realm of conviction.

Faith is produced by the Scriptures which are called "the word of faith" (Rom. 10:8). "So then faith comes by hearing, and hearing by the word of God" (Rom. 10:17). This means Christians who want to develop their faith in God must begin by

learning the basic facts of Scripture. Their knowledge of Scripture must then become the basis upon which they live the Christian life.

WHEN YOU CHANGE YOUR BELIEFS, YOU CHANGE YOUR EXPECTATIONS

The second step in the process of character formation involves changing your beliefs to effect a change in your expectations. Your expectations or vision must come from God's Word. "Where there is no revelation (vision or expectation) the people cast off restraint, but happy is he who keeps the law" (Prov. 29:18).

Some people never change because their belief in God does not create new expectations from God. There are at least six different responses people may have with regard to vision. First, some never see. They have a mechanical problem. Others see it, but don't understand it. They have a mental problem. Still others see, but never pursue the vision. Their problem is with the will. A fourth group sees it, but never feels it. They have an emotional problem. Then there are people who see the vision and through obedience achieve it. The final group sees and shares the vision with followers, demonstrating their leadership capacity.

What expectation has Scripture created in your life? There are four steps to grasp God's vision for your life. First, look within yourself to determine how God has enabled and gifted you. Second, look behind yourself to see how God has used past events to shape you and prepare you for something greater. Then look around yourself to others you admire. I often tell people, "Tell me who your hero is and I'll tell you where you'll be in ten years." Then look ahead to determine where the Lord is leading in your life.

WHEN YOU CHANGE YOUR EXPECTATIONS, YOU CHANGE YOUR ATTITUDE

When you change your expectations, you change your attitude. Your attitude is the predisposition of your life's focus. It may be defined as the habit of your attention. You are on a downward cycle when you develop a "hardening of the attitudes." In contrast, creating positive emotional habits puts you on an upward cycle.

As you consistently apply attitudes, you develop habits that form your character. When a person becomes tired of always being late, he or she may decide to start being on time. As that attitude becomes more prominent in his or her thinking and is more consistently applied, that person begins to develop the habit of punctuality. This new habit helps shape his or her new character.

There are usually four steps involved in developing new attitudes. First, identify the problem you wish to address. In the illustration used above, the problem was chronic lateness. Second, identify the right thinking that will lead to changing an emotional habit. A person decides he or she wants to be on time. The third step involves relating to positive people. We become like those with whom we associate. If we want to become punctual, we should begin associating with people who tend to be punctual. Finally, develop a plan that will encourage positive attitudes and help develop a new habit. Begin by being on time for your next meeting (or class or appointment, etc.), then the next one, and so on. By being on time for one meeting at a time, you will eventually develop the habit of being on time and become known as a punctual person.

WHEN YOU CHANGE YOUR ATTITUDE, YOU CHANGE YOUR ACTIONS

When you change your attitude, you change your actions. The dictionary defines an action as "anything done or performed." Actions may be wrong, ignorant, positive, lucky, planned or unplanned.

Your actions earn your reputation and communicate to others the kind of person you are. "Even a child is known by his deeds, whether what he does is pure and right" (Prov. 20:11). Jesus emphasized this principle by referring to the common practice of identifying a tree by the fruit it produces. "For every tree is known by its own fruit. For men do not gather figs from thorns, nor do they gather grapes from a bramble bush" (Luke 6:44). Our actions are the fruit by which others determine the kind of person we are.

WHEN YOU CHANGE YOUR ACTIONS, YOU CHANGE YOUR HABITS

When you change your actions on a continual basis, you obviously change your accomplishments or habits. An accomplishment is the complete satisfactory outcome of an action. Often this word is used in the positive sense such as when we describe a person who is accomplished in his or her field, i.e. "He is an accomplished surgeon" or "She is an accomplished pianist." Actually, the word means the final outcome regardless of its value, whether it is good or bad. The Scriptures use the word in the sense of carrying something out completely. The goal of the Scriptures is "that the man of God may be complete (accomplished), thoroughly equipped for every good work" (2 Tim. 3:17).

WHEN YOU CHANGE YOUR HABITS, YOU CHANGE YOUR CHARACTER

The purpose of this lesson is to show how to strengthen your character or change for a stronger character. Character is defined as continually doing the right thing, in the right way, with the right attitude, for the right reason because you know it is right.

Many people struggle with gaining control of their time. This problem often manifests itself in arriving late to meetings. Some say being late is a character problem. The persistently late person who changes into a punctual person does so by passing through the process described in the Introduction. First, he or she thinks about the value of punctuality until he or she comes to know that punctuality is a value he or she wants to acquire. He or she begins dreaming about being on time and makes being on time the center of his or her focus. Then action is taken which results in his or her actually being on time for a meeting. As this process is repeated, he or she becomes known as a punctual person. The person's inner character has been changed in this one area.

Let's consider again the process by which we develop character in our life. First, we think it. Then we know it. After that we dream it. We begin to focus on it, then we act on it. That leads to our accomplishing it continually. Ultimately, we become it.

May God help us as we apply this process to developing good habits of the heart.

Chapter 2:

BELIEVING IS KNOWING

RECENTLY, *U.S.A. Today* reported that thirty-eight million Americans smoke. That number is down slightly, reflecting a growing trend among Americans toward a more healthy lifestyle. Although many people have broken their smoking habit, the same article reported that a full seventy percent of those who still smoke want to quit.

Breaking habits remains a significant challenge for many people. Whether it is smoking or some other habit, there are common steps which can and should be taken by those who want to replace a bad habit with a good habit. This chapter talks about breaking habits. Because over twenty-eight million Americans want to quit smoking, we will use the habit of smoking to illustrate this strategy. The habit you want to break in your life may not be smoking. That's all right. The basic principles of this character-building strategy are helpful in breaking any bad habit and replacing it with a corresponding good habit.

Just as a person getting ready to run a marathon must make a mental and emotional decision to get physically fit for the event, so the development of character means total life development. As we apply the principles of character development to our habits, habits which control us today can be brought under control. We do not have to let our bad habits prevent us from becoming all God wants us to be.

CHARACTER MUST BE GROUNDED ON GOD'S PLAN

What is the most ridiculous argument for smoking that you've heard? Some people argue it is all right to smoke because Rebekah "lighted off the camel" (Gen. 24:64). Others claim God approved of smoking, citing the verse "A smoking flax shall he not quench" (Isa. 42:3). Of course, neither of these verses has anything to do with smoking, but they illustrate just how far some people will go to justify their actions.

Believers must study the Bible to determine the principles by which they live. We believe the Bible is the final authority in all matters of faith and practice. This means we should learn how to discern biblical principles which develop character. In developing a godly character, there are several guidelines which will help us as we deal with biblical principles.

Always obey the clear command of Scripture. God calls upon us to "obey the voice of the Lord your God, to keep His commandments and His statutes which are written in the Book of the Law" (Deut. 30:10). An example of such a command in Scripture is found in Ephesians 6:1, "Children, obey your parents in the Lord, for this is right." There can be little doubt in our mind as to the application of this verse in the context of our relationship with our parents. Throughout the Scriptures, there are various clear commands such as this which need to be obeyed.

Avoid any clear negation of Scripture. Just as some Scriptures clearly command specific actions, others just as clearly forbid other actions. An example of this is found in Ephesians 4:31, "Let all bitterness, wrath, anger, clamor, and evil speaking be put away from you, with all malice." This verse strictly forbids bitterness, wrath, anger, clamor, evil speaking and malice in the life of a Christian. Throughout the Scriptures you will find various verses with similar prohibitions.

Avoid all circumstances that may harm your Christian life. Paul reminded the Corinthians, "All things are lawful for me, but all things are not helpful. All things are lawful for me, but I will not be brought under the power of any" (1 Cor. 6:12). Even when no specific Scripture prohibits a behavior pattern or using a substance, Christians should use discernment and avoid anything which may be harmful and/or addictive. This principle applies not only to smoking but to other activities that tend to control people who are engaged in them.

To develop character, be committed to a pure thought life. Jesus taught His disciples, "But I say to you that whoever looks at a woman to lust for her has already committed adultery with her in his heart" (Matt. 5:28). Our behavior, habits and character grow out of our thought life. Therefore, developing a pure thought life is crucial to ultimately developing Christian character. As habits often begin in the mind, breaking bad habits also involves changing our thoughts.

Be careful not to engage in an activity which may cause others to stumble or fall in their Christian life. The first question anyone ever asked God was, "Am I my brother's keeper?" (Gen. 4:9). Although God did not answer Cain on that occasion, the clear teaching of Scripture is that we are responsible for one another. Paul warned the Corinthians, "But beware lest somehow this liberty of yours become a stumbling block to those who are weak" (1 Cor. 8:9). That is also a good warning for us to heed today.

Always obey your conscience. Never violate it. When we begin to compromise our conscience, we are removing one of the checks and balances God has placed in our life to help us overcome temptation to sin. The word "conscience" is derived from two Latin words meaning "to know with." The Bible describes our conscience as the law of God written in our hearts, that accuses us and excuses us when we face and yield to temptation (Rom. 2:15). "Therefore, to him who knows to do good, and does not do it, to him it is sin" (James 4:17).

Avoid activities that intentionally harm your body. When a person becomes a Christian, Christ comes to live in his or her life. When that happens, his or her body becomes the temple of the Holy Spirit and God assumes ownership of the body (1 Cor. 6:19-20). When we engage in any activity as a Christian, we are also involving the temple of God in that activity. Understanding that principle has certain specific moral implications. Paul urged the Corinthians, "Flee sexual immorality. Every sin that a man does is outside the body, but he who commits sexual immorality sins against his own body" (1 Cor. 6:18).

Never do anything that cannot be carried out in faith. The first designation by which Christians were identified was "believers" because faith is at the heart of everything it means to be a Christian. Acting outside the realm of faith is a dysfunctional behavior pattern for Christians. "He who doubts is condemned if he eats, because he does not eat from faith; for whatever is not from faith is sin" (Rom. 14:23).

HOW TO DETERMINE BIBLICAL PRINCIPLES

As you study the Scriptures, be careful to discern biblical principles before attempting to apply them to life. A young lady determined God wanted her to break a relationship with Paul so she could marry Mark on the basis of Psalm 37:37 which reads in part "Mark the blameless (perfect) man." Of course, her interpretation and application of the verse had nothing to do with the intended meaning of the passage. If she had taken the time to discern the principle and apply that to her situation, she may have dumped Mark for Paul and ended up with a much better marriage.

By their nature, principles are transcultural. When Jesus told His disciples, "Do not go into the way of the Gentiles, and do not enter a city of the Samaritans" (Matt. 10:5), He was telling them to remain focused on their mission of reaching "the lost sheep of the house of Israel" (Matt. 10:6). As we seek to reach people in our community today, most of those we meet will be Gentiles. If we apply the principle of remaining focused on reaching our target group, our behavior pattern will be opposite of that of the disciples. Cultures change, but the eternal principles of God can be applied in every culture.

Principles must also be transtemporal, i.e. not limited to a specific era in time. When Paul taught the Romans about their response to civil authority, he reminded them "for he does not bear the sword in vain" (Rom. 13:4). This meant God had established civil authority and empowered them to inflict punishment appropriate for the crime committed. Most law enforcement officers today no longer carry swords as the Roman soldiers did. While the eternal principle applies today, its expression looks different in our time. Today we might say, "for he does not bear arms in vain" (Rom. 13:4, ELT).

As you look for biblical principles, learn to look beyond the actual to the principle. Jesus told his disciples, "And whoever compels you to go one mile, go with him two" (Matt. 5:41). This does not mean He expected His disciples to cast off the burden of the Romans at the two-mile marker rather than the one-mile marker. Rather, the principle is that Christians should be willing to go above and beyond the realm of duty in their relationships with others.

Because our character is grounded on our thinking or understanding, it is important that we learn how to think about the Bible. First, think about the Bible with a yielded spirit. We should always approach the Scriptures willing to let God speak to us rather than attempting to force God to say what we want. Second, ask the Holy Spirit to teach you. Jesus promised the Holy Spirit would "teach you all things, and bring to your remembrance all things that I said to you" (John 14:26). Third, think practically. Ask God how you can apply each principle you discover to your life. Finally, think holy. As you read the Scriptures, look for ways you can become like God.

HOW TO INTERPRET THE BIBLE

When God inspired people to write the Scriptures, He arranged for them to use words which could be understood by those who would read and hear the Scriptures. When we study the Bible, we should apply David Cooper's Golden Rule of Interpretation when attempting to determine the meaning of a verse or passage. This rule states, "When the plain sense of Scripture makes common sense, seek no other sense, but take every word at its primary literal meaning."

When we interpret the Bible literally, we are attempting to determine what the Scriptures meant to those who wrote and first read it. This means we should interpret the Scriptures in light of the historical context or background of the passage being considered. Also, the passage should be interpreted in light of the author's original plan and purpose. This means a verse should always be interpreted within the context in which it appears with special attention given to the author's use of words and their meaning in the culture in which the passage was written.

PRINCIPLES TO GROW CHARACTER

Several biblical principles should be broadly applied in life as we seek to break bad habits and develop godly character. The first is the *love principle*. When properly motivated by love, you will respect people and the law. When we love others, we are fulfilling the "royal law" (James 2:8). Therefore we are motivated to do right because we love others. In the context of a smoker attempting to break that habit, he or she is motivated to do so because he or she does not want to harm others by secondhand smoke.

The second biblical principle to be widely applied in our life is the *loyalty principle*. This principle states our yieldedness to Christ motivates us to do right in order that we might please Him. In the context of breaking the smoking habit, some people quit smoking out of their desire to follow the Lord more completely.

The *education principle* is a third principle which needs to be widely applied in our life. This principle states that we do right because of what we have learned. When some people learn how smoking affects their health, they have a greater motivation to quit smoking than they did previously.

Fourth, the *training principle* states that we do right because we have done right so many times that it has become a way of life for us. The reverse is also true. This means habits like smoking which are developed over long periods of time tend to take a long time to break. The key is not to quit smoking forever, but rather to quit smoking today. When that is accomplished, you can quit smoking for another day, then another. Before long, the days add into weeks which add into months and you are no longer a smoker. An impossible habit can be broken, one day at a time.

A fifth principle is the *reward principle*. People tend to do right because of the innate satisfaction it gives. As you break the smoking habit, the food you eat begins to taste better and eating meals becomes more enjoyable. Also, money previously spent on tobacco is now available for other interests. As we connect these rewards in our thinking to breaking the habit, we are more highly motivated to quit smoking.

A sixth principle to apply is the *punishment principle* which states we do right because of the consequences associated with doing wrong. One man struggled with smoking until his doctor warned him he would have a major heart attack within five years if he did not quit immediately. Being confronted with the consequences of his actions not only helped him quit smoking, but also helped him deal with other unhealthy aspects of his lifestyle.

Finally, the *fear principle* states that we do right because of the unsettling emotions we feel when we do wrong. Often, when people try to break a habit like smoking, they will periodically lapse into their previous lifestyle. When this happens, they usually have an emotional response to their lapse. This unsettled feeling should help them remember why they are trying to quit smoking and begin the process again.

One of our responsibilities as Christians is to develop correct character. God calls us to "pursue peace with all people, and holiness, without which no one will see the Lord" (Heb. 12:14). A godly character is based on right thinking about God and His purposes for our life. Then we must apply the principles of the Word of God to our life as we cooperate with the Spirit of God in developing godly character in our life.

Chapter 3:

ATTITUDE ADJUSTMENTS

T HE future belongs to those who believe in the beauty of their dreams," according to Eleanor Roosevelt. People who prove most successful in life are those who believe their dreams can be realized. They have an attitude of success which is able to face and overcome the immense obstacles normally faced by all who would dare to dream and turn their dreams to reality. They understand their "altitude" in life depends upon the "attitude" with which they face the challenges of life. Zig Ziglar puts it this way, "Your attitude is more important than your aptitude."

The development of character will become the basis for success in all you do. The person with character has learned to constantly do the right thing, in the right way, with the right attitude, for the right purpose because he or she knows it is right. According to our character-building paradigm, (1) when we change our thinking, we change our convictions; (2) when we change our convictions, we change our vision; (3) when we change our vision, we change our attitudes; (4) when we change our attitudes, we change our actions; (5) when we change our actions, we change our habits; (6) when we change our habits, we change our life/character.

Our attitudes can have a positive or negative impact on our character. Unfortunately, for too many people, their wrong attitude leads to weak character. They express this wrong attitude by making excuses. They express the attitude of irresponsibility with claims such as, "It's not my responsibility." They express the attitude of being unaccountable with claims such as, "No one will see me do it." They express something of their own apathy when they claim, "No one cares if I do it." They express an attitude that is sure to produce weak character when they compromise their values on the basis that everyone else is doing it.

PROPER ATTITUDES DEVELOP CHARACTER

Just as poor attitude can result in weak character, so right attitudes help develop a strong and good character. I often encourage my students to become leaders by studying influence. Let me ask you a question. Who has had a significant impact on your life? Once you have identified several people who have influenced you, then ask, "What characteristic of these people most influenced me?" When I ask this question to groups, a few people identify individuals who taught them some life skill which has changed their life. Others identify people to whom they were attracted physically. By far the greatest part of the group usually identifies someone whose positive attitude was contagious.

The greatest people in the world have the greatest attitude. According to Eric Butterworth, "Nothing stops the man who desires to achieve. Every obstacle is simply a course to develop his achievement muscle. It's a strengthening of his powers of accomplishment." Great leaders overcome great obstacles to achieve significant success. When I profiled ten men who had established new churches, I called the book, *Getting a Church Started in the Face of Insurmountable Odds with Limited Resources in Unlikely Circumstances.*

One of America's greatest presidents became a living illustration of this truth during his lifetime. In 1831, his business failed. The next year he was defeated in an election for a seat in the legislature. This was followed a year later by another business failure. In 1836, he suffered a nervous breakdown. From 1838 through 1858, he unsuccessfully ran for office in seven different elections in an attempt to become a congressman, senator and vice president. But in 1860, Abraham Lincoln was elected president of the United States. Lincoln told others, "Always bear in mind that your own resolution to succeed is more important than any other one thing."

What is the key to success in the workplace? In recent years, much study has been done in this field. The Carnegie Institute conducted a study which concluded that success in the workplace is about fifteen percent dependent upon skills and about eighty-five percent dependent upon personality. This conclusion is supported by the myriad of business books being published which link success in business with attitudes like excellence and adaptability rather than accounting practices or technological breakthroughs. Your personality is formed by attitudes and grows out of your character.

The importance of our attitude and personality in the context of achieving personal success in life is also emphasized in another set of statistics. Studies conducted to determine why individuals are fired suggest about a third (thirty-five percent) were fired because of incompetence, i.e. they failed to consistently perform well. In contrast, over half (fifty-three percent) were fired because of a personality-related problem. All other reasons combined only accounted for twenty-seven percent of those fired. Apart from incompetence, a person is twice as likely to be fired for an attitude problem than all other problems combined.

You cannot determine your circumstances, but when you have the right attitude you get the best out of your circumstances and rise above circumstances. People with the wrong attitude complain, "Why me? Why this? Why now?" You cannot determine your emotional response, but when you have the right attitude, you can rise above your feelings. You cannot stop feelings, but you can keep your feelings from stopping you.

BAD ATTITUDES HINDER CONTINUOUS SUCCESS

Bad attitudes will hinder one's ongoing success in at least five ways. First, a negative attitude tends to sour one's confidence. Second, bad attitudes can misdirect your efforts. Third, they will inevitably dilute one's stamina and commitment to purpose. Fourth, bad attitudes will jam one's efforts in planning. Finally, a negative attitude tends to cut one off from help.

There is an element of truth in the maxim, "You are what you think you are." If you think you are beaten, you are. If you think you dare not, you don't. If you'd like to win, but think you can't, it's almost certain you won't. First, you conceive, then you achieve. You may not accomplish all you dream of doing, but those who have no dreams never fall short of their expectations.

WE ARE RESPONSIBLE FOR OUR ATTITUDES

To achieve ongoing success in life and build strong character, we must learn we are responsible for our attitudes. Too often people attempt to deny responsibility by making excuses. When their marriage fails, they excuse it by claiming they married wrong or, it was all their spouse's fault. People stagnate in their job and blame their job, i.e. they don't like it. Thomas Edison once said, "Opportunity is missed by most people because it is dressed in overalls and looks like work." Students adopt the same attitude about their studies. It is easy to find excuses. We can blame our dysfunctional families, the injustices in our society or the fact we were born on the wrong side of the tracks. But those who make it in life refuse to use excuses to justify a bad attitude.

For the Christian, a lousy attitude is not an option. "But the fruit of the Spirit is love, joy, peace, longsuffering, kindness, goodness, faithfulness, gentleness, self-control. Against such there is no law" (Gal. 5:22-23). These are the characteristics of a positive attitude which builds strong character. Because this is what the Holy Spirit is doing in our life today, we can know God will help us change.

What kind of attitude tends to characterize you most of the time. The pessimist complains about the wind. The optimist expects a better wind. But the person with character changes the sail. Someone has said, "Don't wait for your ship to come in; swim out to it."

God wants us to take control of our attitude and control our thoughts. As Joshua prepared to assume the role of leader of Israel after the death of Moses, God told him, "Constantly remind the people about these laws, and you yourself must think about them everyday and every night so that you will be sure to obey all of them. For only then will you succeed. Yes, be bold and strong! Banish fear and doubt! For remember the Lord your God is with you wherever you go" (Josh. 1:8-9, LB).

Why do people do good? At least three motives control our decision to do right. Some are motivated *extrinsically* by an outward motivation. They work hard for the recognition of others, a prize to be won or a bonus to be earned. Others are motivated intrinsically by an inner drive. For them there is a satisfaction connected with a task completed or a job done well. For the Christian, there is a third kind of motivation, a *Christocentric* motivation in life. The apostle Paul wrote, "For me to live is Christ" (Phil. 1:21). In the same epistle he added, "I can do all things through Christ who strengthens me" (Phil. 4:13).

WE MUST CHOOSE GOOD ATTITUDES

There is much in life over which we have no control, but we can always control the attitude with which we face the challenges God has placed before us. My good friend John Maxwell says, "Life is a choice!" By this he means our quality of life depends on the attitudes we choose to face life's challenges.

God chooses what you will go through; you choose how you will go through it. A. L. Williams claims, "Life is ten percent what you make it and ninety percent how you take it." When faced with a situation which seems unfair or larger than we can handle, we can be confident that God thinks we can handle it. "No temptation (problem in life) has overtaken you except such as is common to man; but God is faithful, who will not allow you to be tempted beyond what you are able, but with the temptation will also make the way of escape, that you may be able to bear it" (1 Cor. 10:13).

Our choices are important, especially when it comes to choosing an attitude with which to face our problems. C. S. Lewis explained, "Every time you make a choice, you are turning the control part of you into something a little different from what it was before. And taking your life as a whole, with all its innumerable choices, you are slowly turning the control thing either into a heavenly creature or into a hellish one."

Our attitudes are very important in the process of developing a godly character. The good news is that we can change our attitudes. We can choose to face the challenges of life in reliance upon the faithfulness of God. We do not have to have a fatalistic "poor me" attitude toward problems in life. We can determine the strength of our faith, love, joy, peace, humility, kindness, and self-discipline. May God help each of us make the right choices and approach life with the right attitude.

Chapter 4:

BASIS FOR SUCCESS IN CHRISTIAN LIFE AND SERVICE

"YOUR actions speak so loud I can't hear what you are saying." Perhaps you have heard this common complaint made against someone. Maybe you have thought it yourself about someone whose message tends to be contradicted by his or her lifestyle. People resent being told to do something by people who do not "practice what they preach." Rather, they model the behavior they witness rather than the lesson they hear.

Parents see this principle work out in the life of their children. Children model the behavior of those around them including their parents. Unfortunately, they don't discern between the good habits we would like them to learn and the bad habits we hope they don't develop. A father complained about his children leaving their shoes in a hallway when he stubbed his toe on a shoe one evening. Although he had seen his children leaving their shoes in the hall on previous occasions, when he turned on the light he discovered he had just kicked one of his own shoes. He realized his children were doing what he did rather than what he said.

Our actions not only affect our family, they impact every area of our Christian life and ministry. Gifted men and women in ministry have failed to achieve their potential in ministry because they lack character. Others achieve initial success but their character undermines their ministry and they experience a significant long-term decline in effectiveness. The development of biblical character is the basis for success in your Christian life and service.

This being the case, the question most pressing for those striving for success in their Christian life and service is, "What is character?" A good dictionary will define character as "moral excellence and firmness" or "moral constitution." Our character is our predisposition to right attitudes and right actions based on right reasons. It is the focus of our actions or the habit that guides our behavior. Our character is the controlling values of our personality.

There is an open debate concerning the relationship between good character and good behavior. Which comes first? Which is the cause and which is the effect? To some extent they influence each other. Our character grows out of our behavior, but then it influences future behavior. We become what we do which causes us to keep on doing what we are.

Character motivates us to do right for the right reasons. Not everyone who does right does so for the same reasons. Some people do right because they have never done wrong. Others do right because they don't know how to do wrong. Still others do right because they are afraid they will be caught if they do wrong. Still others do right in hope of earning a reward. Finally, there are those who do right because their friends do right. Which of these is acting out of a biblical character? The person with character has learned to consistently do the right thing with the right attitude for the biblical purpose.

COMPARISON OF RIGHT AND LEFT PERSONS

John Maxwell says, "The person with character has the ability to carry out a decision long after the emotions that influenced the choice are gone." By this he medals a person of character does right even when he doesn't feel like doing right. Many people can be caught up in the enthusiasm of a dream and begin working toward its realization, but only people of character have what it takes to keep on working toward that goal when the zeal of the moment has passed and getting the job done takes hard work.

Psychologists have identified two thinking patterns based on the theory that the two sides of the human brain tend to operate differently. The left side of the brain tends to be emotionally based whereas the right side of the brain tends to be rationale based. The differences between left-side people and right-side people can be seen by the different responses they have when making a decision in a common situation

Left-side people ask the question, "What is easiest?" Right-side people ask the question, "What is right?"

Left-side people take the approach, "When I feel good, then I'll do it." Right-side people take the approach, "When I do it, then I'll feel good."

Left-side people are controlled by moods. Right-side people are controlled by priorities.

Left-side people tend to have a selfish or self-centered mind set. Right-side people tend to have a servant or others-oriented mind set.

Left-side people have a lifestyle that disagrees with what they say. The lifestyle and message of right-side people tends to harmonize well.

Left-side people tend to look for excuses. Right-side people tend to look for solutions.

Left-side people are outwardly influenced. Right-side people are inwardly motivated.

Left-side people tend to quit during the tough times. Right-side people tend to continue during the tough times.

Left-side people tend to whine. Right-side people tend to win.

Maxwell concludes, "Right-side people will have long-lasting friendships, successful marriages, satisfying vocations, and an inward happiness." People who want ongoing success in their Christian life and service are people who want to move from the left side to the right side in the way they approach the challenges of life.

HOW TO STEP FROM THE LEFT TO THE RIGHT SIDE

How then can one move from the left side to the right side? When you look at the description of left- and right-side people, the contrast between where you are and where you want to be may seem so great that you struggle with believing such a change is possible. Perhaps the change is too great to make right now, but you can take several steps that will help you achieve that change in a more manageable manner.

Begin by learning the power of decision. Make a personal commitment to develop character. When Jesus called on people to follow Him, He said, "If anyone desires to come after Me, let him deny himself, and take up his cross daily, and follow Me" (Luke 9:23). The successful Christian life begins with a decision to be a disciple of Jesus Christ.

A century ago, a highly successful British pastor told his students, "Do right though the stars fall." Charles Haddon Spurgeon was pastor of one of the world's largest churches and president of a school that trained men to begin churches throughout England and in other parts of the world. He learned from his own experience and that of others that success comes to those who focus on the right reasons for all they do regardless of the circumstances around them. Jesus emphasized this principle when He told His disciples, "But seek first the kingdom of God and His righteousness, and all these things shall be added to you" (Matt. 6:33).

Third, establish the habit of doing things that are right. You can do what you want to do, and you can do it well. The apostle Paul urged the Colossians, And whatever you do, do it heartily, as to the Lord and not to men" (Col. 3:23).

A fourth step in moving from the left side to the right side involves changing your focus and becoming others oriented. General William Booth, founder of the Salvation Army, considered this principle so important that he once sent a single-word telegram to the International Convention of the Salvation Army because he was too sick to attend. The word was "others." He knew his movement would only experience on-going success as they lived to meet needs in other people's lives. He attempted to develop the attitude of Jesus in the lives of his followers. Jesus said, "But I say to you, love your enemies, bless those who curse you, do good to those who hate you, and pray for those who spitefully use you and persecute you ... For if you love those who love you, what reward have you? Do not even the tax collectors do the same? And if you greet your brethren only, what do you do more than others? Do not even the tax collectors do so?" (Matt. 5:44, 46-47).

Fifth, be firm in your commitment, but patient and flexible with your inability to do all you desire. Many of us struggle with the reality of our mortality. We must learn to use the gifts and abilities God has given us to accomplish His will, and be willing to let God use others to do what we cannot do. The prophet Jeremiah struggled with his inability to speak and his youth when God called him to his prophetic ministry (Jer. 1:6). The Lord responded, "Do not say, 'I am a youth,' for you shall go to all to whom I send you, and whatever I command you, you shall speak" (Jer. 1:7). God promised to enable Jeremiah to accomplish the task given him. We can claim similar help from God today in becoming what God wants us to be.

Verbalize your principles so that you remember your expectations and how to apply them. Write them out in statements. God told Habakkuk, "Write the vision and make it plain on tablets, that he may run who reads it" (Hab. 2:2). This means God wanted Habakkuk to make his message so clear people would run to do it.

Step seven involves developing a track record which becomes the standard by which you make important decisions in life. When confronted with the problems and decisions of life, begin by looking first to your principles. Then gather all the facts you can. Only after you have gathered data and identified your principles can you begin applying those principles to the challenge facing you to implement a workable solution. This is the process by which we move toward maturity in our Christian life. Paul told his followers, "I press toward the goal for the prize of the upward call of God in Christ Jesus. Therefore let us, as many as are mature, have this mind; and if in anything you think otherwise, God will reveal even this to you" (Phil. 3:14-15).

Finally, build upon initial success to gain confidence and build a godly character. "Hope deferred makes the heart sick, but when the desire comes, it is a tree of life" (Prov. 13:12). This means that success in accomplishing our goals will produce new energy to produce even greater things. Remember Paul's reminder to the Philippians of the strength available to accomplish our goals. "I can do all things through Christ who strengthens me" (Phil. 4:13).

Chapter 5:

DEALING WITH CHANGE
AND GROWTH

EVERY new day is an opportunity to change and grow into what God wants us to be. That means today you have the opportunity of moving one step closer to God's ultimate goal for your life. Because change may be either good or bad, it also means you have the opportunity of moving away from God's goal for your life today.

Someone has said, "Nothing is constant in life but change." The apostle Paul reminded the Romans that God is constantly engaged in the process of changing us "to be conformed to the image of His Son" (Rom. 8:29). He expressed his confidence to the Philippians "that He who has begun a good work in you will complete it until the day of Jesus Christ" (Phil. 1:6). We too can have this confidence that the Holy Spirit is constantly working change in our life to accomplish God's goal for our life and make us all He wants us to be.

But what about our part? Does character come naturally as God works in our life or do we have to make changes to get character? The law of the division of labor teaches us that in many areas of life, God expects us to do what we can do while He does what only He can do. That biblical principle certainly applies in this case. When we grow, we change. We grow in character when we make decisions based on what we know, and it affects our feelings. We cannot grow without change, but we can change without growth. Growth is changing toward a goal.

Change is much easier said than done. Everyone wants to change for the better. Everyone admires the person who has changed for the better. But comparatively few people actually make a significant change for the better. The people who do so are growing in character.

THE WRONG WAY TO CHANGE

Many people are resistant to change. Even the words we use to describe change discourage people from changing. The dictionary describes change as being "different." When you look up the word "different" in the dictionary, it is defined simply as "not normal." Most people do not want to be described as "not normal."

Even when people overcome this initial hurdle, often their approach to change is wrong and hinders their potential growth. Some ask God to change their habits. Others look to

God to change their circumstances. Still others ask God to change the people around them. A better approach is to ask God to change their basic approach to life. When we change our approach to life, God can change others around us. This makes us agents of change in our sphere of influence.

Another common problem people struggle with when they attempt to make significant change and grow involves changing the wrong things. Some take a legalistic approach to life and attempt to change their actions without changing their thinking. Others experiment, making changes to test the results but not committing themselves to making permanent adjustments. For others, change is just cosmetic. They make changes on the outside but nothing changes inside. And then there are those who struggle to be decisive but continually change their thinking. This usually results in a state of general confusion. A fifth group focuses on outward results but fails to make the inner changes necessary to accomplish their goal. They try to change their fruit without changing their root.

PEOPLE WITH CHARACTER

People with character are people who have learned to manage change in their life and use it wisely to achieve lasting and significant growth toward God's goal for their life. They have learned five important lessons in life that help them turn transitions into growth experiences. These five principles outline the steps necessary to manage change that encourages the development of character in our life.

The first step involves having a deep personal desire to realize personal growth and development. The apostle Paul was motivated by the desire, "that I may know Him and the power of His resurrection, and the fellowship of His sufferings, being conformed to His death" (Phil. 3:10). This kind of desire provides the motivation needed to do what is necessary to accomplish the goal. A football coach put it this way. "The will to win is important. The will to prepare to win is not only vital, it is imperative."

The second step involves a strategy for growth and change. People who change usually know how to change and therefore they know how to grow. This was true in Paul's life. He wrote, "Brethren, I do not count myself to have apprehended; but one thing I do, forgetting those things which are behind and reaching forward to those things which are ahead, I press toward the goal for the prize of the upward call of God in Christ Jesus" (Phil. 3:13-14). He was so committed to change and personal growth that he urged others to follow his example. "The things which you learned and received and heard and saw in me, these do, and the God of peace will be with you" (Phil. 4:9).

To change, people need both a goal and strategy for change, and they need to know the difference between these two important elements of a growth plan. A goal focuses upon an outward result while a strategy deals with the inward process. The goal may be defined as the prize, but the strategy is the road that leads to that prize. Goals tend to be temporary, changing once they have been achieved. Strategies tend to be more permanent, often continuing long after the initial goal has been achieved. Our goals reflect our changing motivation, but the strategy by which we achieve those goals becomes the driving force in our life.

Step three in the process of change involves eliminating burdens and barriers. The Christian life demands that we "lay aside every weight, and the sin which so easily ensnares us" that we may run with endurance (Heb. 12:1). As we run that race, we do so "looking unto Jesus" (Heb. 12:2). We must set aside hindrances and focus on the right goal.

Every child is beauty and the beast. Just as it takes two wings to fly, it takes two forces to produce balance in the child's life. They need both our love and discipline. Love brings out the best in them. Discipline curbs that destructive nature which may harm the child or allow the child to harm others. Likewise, in the Christian life, we need both negative and positive discipline. Negatively, we need to get rid of distractions, weights, and hindrances. Positively, we need to become focused in life.

Step four in this process is to learn how to overcome failure. Failure does not have to destroy you unless you allow your attitude toward failure stop you. All of us have outer problems and inner disappointments, but people of character have a strong will to face and overcome their failures. Thomas Edison failed many times before succeeding at inventing the incandescent light bulb.

There is a difference between saying, "I failed" and "I am a failure." All of us have failed, but that does not make us failures. Don't wear failure like a suit. Rather, recognize failure for what it is, part of the journey to success. All of us failed to meet God's standard of holiness, but "Christ Jesus came into the world to save sinners" that we might reach heaven successfully (1 Tim. 1:15). Don't let your failures control you. Take control of your failures.

In his book, *The Screwtape Letters*, C. S. Lewis has a senior demon advise a junior demon, "Get Christians preoccupied with failure. From there on the battle is won." Unfortunately, this strategy has been all too successful. When many Christians fail, they become so focused on their failure they are demotivated to try again. In contrast, most millionaires lose money before they make money.

If we are going to grow to become all God wants us to be, we need to learn from every failure. While Alexander Graham Bell was attempting to make a hearing aid for his deaf sister, one of his failed experiments resulted in the telephone. We need to take responsibility for our failures and not use failure as an excuse.

The fifth step in our strategy to manage change and grow in character is to have a dream or vision of what God wants to accomplish in your life. Does the person with vision go after character, or does the person with principles gravitate to purpose in life? Actually, there is truth in both assumptions. Vision and character tend to be developed together. People with character but no vision become examples for others. People with vision but no character are often very productive in what they attempt, but may not be a positive role model. But when both character and vision are present, they tend to multiply effectiveness.

To have great dreams and character, we must learn to live outside ourselves. People with character live by principles outside themselves. People with vision are motivated to goals outside themselves.

When we have a vision, it moves us to actualize its potential. First we visualize, then we actualize. When our vision grows out of our character, we see exactly how to make it happen and have the power and principles to make it happen. Then we become effective managers of change, resulting in significant growth toward God's goal for our life.

Today, there is an opportunity for you to change and grow into what God wants you to be. May God help you today and every day to pass through the changes of life so your habits become habits of the heart.

Chapter 6:

HABITS OF THE HEART

THE title of this book and this chapter is taken from writings of Tocqueville. In the early days of our nation, Tocqueville traveled from his native France to America to learn the secret of our national greatness. He concluded America was great because America was good. He used the expression "habits of the heart" to describe America's virtue, character, and morals.

The dictionary defines habit as "a behavior pattern acquired by frequent repetition that is reflected in regular or increased performance of your life." It is derived from a Latin root meaning "clothing that is usually worn." In some cases, this term is still used in English when referring to a nun's or monk's habit. Even when not used with literal reference to clothes, the metaphor still applies. Our habits are the practices we wrap around our life. Just as a nun is recognized by her habit, so also our habits form the reputation by which we are known.

No one is without habits. Habits may be voluntary or involuntary, good or bad. A good habit involves doing the right thing for the right purpose on a continual basis. Our habits, both good and bad, extend to every part of our life. We may have good language habits like expressing thanks to others, or we may have bad language habits like cursing. Our emotional habits may be positive such as laughter or may be negative such as the practice of rolling one's eyes. Some habits are physical, such as covering our mouth when we cough (good habit) or burping loudly in public (bad habit). Some habits tend to be instinctive. When we drive our car after driving for many years, we do so instinctively. Some people struggle with stuttering which may be an instinctive habit.

As a child, my mother often told me, "If you do right, you'll be right." She understood the key to her son developing a good character involved getting him into the habit of doing the right things. She wanted me to get into the habit of responding properly to what has been learned.

HOW TO RESPOND TO OUR WORLD

Our habits are the ways we typically respond to our world on the basis of what we have learned. Habits are not formed by a single response to a unique situation. Rather, as we repeatedly respond in a similar manner to things around us, we develop habits. Our habits are the responses of our personality to our world and, as such, grow out of different levels of our thinking and feeling.

Our habits begin in our mind with the way we think about the world. This involves three aspects of our ability to think. First, we remember how we have faced similar situations in the past. Remembering is the ability to recreate the past and relate it to the present. Second, we anticipate a similar set of circumstances arising in the present. Anticipating is the ability to predict a response or situation that will occur in the future. Third, we imagine a similar response to a situation which has not yet come to pass. Imagining is the ability to conceive responses or situations that is not yet related to the present.

Our habits also affect the way we perceive the world. Perception also involves three steps. First, we receive data. This involves both receiving and understanding information. Second, we interpret data. This gives meaning to facts and classifies them with other information. Third, we respond to data. The data we have received and interpreted helps us respond in a certain way. The cat that sits on a hot stove once will never sit on another hot stove. The same cat will also avoid sitting on a cold stove.

Our habits also influence the way we feel about the world. Emotions are the response of our bodily state to a situation. Emotions may be expressed in anger, fear, alienation or depression. Feelings are also the expression of our bodily state. We may feel happy, strained, pressured or excited.

HOW TO BREAK A HABIT!

A habit is formed by repetition. Our constant repetition of an attitude or action results in both good and bad habits. Some people think there is no such thing as a new habit. They argue the best we can hope for is to simply modify some old habit. But just as our old habits were once new habits, so we can develop new good habits to replace the old bad habits we no longer want. There are ten steps involved in breaking old habits and forming new habits in our life.

Step one involves knowing and understanding our situation and condition in life. Many people attempt to break habits without taking this first step. Paul realized the importance of this step in the process of achieving meaningful change in his life. He acknowledged, "For I know that in me (that is, in my flesh) nothing good dwells; for to will is present with me, but how to perform what is good I do not find" (Rom. 7:18).

Once we understand our situation, step two involves taking a closer look at ourselves. This involves an awareness of both our strengths and weaknesses. As Paul struggled to overcome sin in his life, he acknowledged, "For the good that I will to do, I do not do; but the evil I will not to do, that I practice" (Rom. 7:19).

The third step in breaking a habit involves evaluation. This involves measuring the intensity of the negative influences in your life. The apostle Paul understood the consequences of the sin with which he struggled in his own life (Rom. 7:19).

This step is followed by visualizing. Visualizing involves forming an image of the ideal behavior that you desire. Often, I tell my students, "Tell me who your hero is and I'll tell what you will be like." Paul visualized victory over sin before it became a part of his experience. He wrote, "For sin shall not have dominion over you, for you are not under law but under grace."

Next, position yourself. See the result that will come to you for eliminating negative habits. Paul's victory over sin was based on his position "in Christ." "For the law of the Spirit of life in Christ Jesus has made me free from the law of sin and death" (Rom. 8:2).

The sixth step in this process is to want it. This involves creating and feeling a desire to realize these ideals. In discussing our struggle for victory over sin, Paul wrote, "Likewise you also, reckon yourselves to be dead indeed to sin, but alive to God in Christ Jesus our Lord" (Rom. 6:11).

Next, reach for it. Look outside yourself for vision, strength, and help. We can break habits which are too big for us when we rely upon God and let Him work freely in our life. "Now may the God of peace Himself sanctify you completely; and may your whole spirit, soul, and body be preserved blameless at the coming of our Lord Jesus Christ" (1 Thess. 5:23).

Step eight involves making a choice. We must make a definite and deliberate decision to change before we will overcome our habit. Then, we must act on that decision. The ninth step in this process involves being engaged persistently in the desired response. "Test all things, hold fast what is good" (1 Thess. 5:21).

Finally, we break habits by faith. Trust God to complete the action you have begun. "He who calls you is faithful, who also will do it" (1 Thess. 5:24).

May God help you develop good habits of the heart.

Chapter 7:

VALUES AND MORALITY

ONE of the great challenges facing parents and youth workers today involves values training. The task of passing on moral values to the next generation may never have been as difficult as it is today. While this is true for many groups within American society, it is especially true for those of us committed to traditional Christian values. There are forces within American society today which appear openly hostile to those values reflected in the Ten Commandments and the Sermon on the Mount.

When William Kilpatrick wrote *Why Johnny Cannot Tell Right from Wrong*, this respected Catholic layman attacked cultural relativism. He noted that nondirected methods of moral education which urge students to make equally valid choices in the jungle of relativism have actually encouraged youth to experiment with drugs, sex, and lawlessness. The new approach to teaching morality is called "values clarification." Essentially, this involves doing what you want to or like to do rather than what you ought to do. As a result of years of values clarification, we now have a generation of young people who have never been confronted with moral absolutes.

The title of this book, *The Habits of the Heart*, is taken from an expression used by Tocqueville to describe the reason for America's greatness. Tocqueville concluded America was great because America was good. But few would believe Tocqueville would come to the same conclusion today if he were to evaluate contemporary American society. Something significant has changed, especially during the last half of the Twentieth Century.

SOURCES OF EROSION IN AMERICAN MORAL

Among the several factors which have eroded away at traditional moral values is a changing culture. In the late sixties, Harvey Cox wrote *The Secular City* which described our changing culture in four pictures. The first picture was that of the tribe, a group of people bound together by a common language and currency. As the tribe develops, it becomes a town. The difference between a tribe and town in Cox's paradigm was industry.

The further development of the town results in the metropolis. The two phenomena which best describe the metropolis is the switchboard and the cloverleaf. The switchboard is the key to the extensive communications network and the cloverleaf is the key to the extensive transportation network of the metropolis. Ultimately, a metropolis may grow into a megalopolis. This fourth picture describes the explosion of the world-class super cities. The values of the megalopolis differ significantly from those of the tribe.

In addition to the sociological changes which normally accompany urban growth, other influences have impacted our national moral values. Immigration policies have welcomed many to America who have introduced their conflicting values to our society. Also, public schools which once taught traditional American values to students no longer serve as a conduit of morality. This change has been accompanied by a widespread perception within our society that the Bible is at best a myth rather than a source of morality. Unfortunately, American churches have largely failed to challenge these changes in our national moral ethic. Rather, they have retreated from effective teaching (*didache*) and preaching (the *kerygma*).

FOUR SOURCES OF MORALITY

In the past, moral values were communicated to a generation through the churches and schools. Today, these institutions are largely ineffective in communicating traditional moral values to a new generation of Americans. How then are moral values transferred in society today? In his book, *The Lonely Crowd*, author David Reisman suggests four sources from which moral values and character are transmitted.

The first source of moral values training may be described as "tradition-directed." This is perhaps best represented in immigrant families which communicate their old-world values to their new-world children. The children of Irish Catholic, Scandinavian, Oriental, Hispanic, African, and other immigrants are taught to value their heritage and continue the traditions of their family. The St. Patrick's Day parade, Chinese Restaurants, and the taco are examples of how other cultural values have been imported into American society. Unfortunately, some of the other values imported by American immigrants have been less positive.

In this model of values training, the culture is the authority upon which values are based. The immigrant becomes the role model for first generation American children. The weakness of this approach to values training include (1) the absence of an outward biblical standard, (2) conflict with traditional American values, (3) the absence of an absolute standard which often results in conflict with other ethnic groups, (4) the inability to reproduce itself once it has been removed from its original culture, and (S) problems associated with differences in clothing, language, music, and other outward expressions of culture. As a result, this approach to values training often fails within the first generational transition. The culture is not preserved to the second and third generations as was intended by the original immigrant parents.

The second approach to values training may be described as "inner-directed." This approach is represented by traditional Protestant American values which are an amalgamation of biblical ethics, American "worth of the individual," and republicanism. These prize justice (do right), success (get ahead), and freedom (individualism).

In this approach, the authority rests in the Bible. People like Benjamin Franklin and Abraham Lincoln became the role models. A new generation was encouraged to pattern their lives after these heroes. But this approach also has its weakness. Those who take this approach to values training often develop an attitude of superiority and expect everyone to live by their values. Those who conform outwardly without adopting the values themselves then become guilty of legalism. This approach accentuates inner conflicts with the negative side of our human nature. Openness and acceptance of other values become the seeds of its destruction.

The third approach to values training may be described as "non-driven." The key to understanding this approach is in the relationship between a stimulus and a response. This approach causes people to conform to the pressures of others. As a result, they give in to the lower urges of their personality. This approach is taken by those who backslide out of the tradition-directed and inner-directed paradigms discussed above and those who drop out of culture completely. It often resembles a blend of other approaches to communicating values.

In this approach, human lust or the old nature is the authority from which values are derived. The popular culture provides role models like Madonna and Michael Jackson. This approach to communicating values is also plagued with weakness. The values communicated are motivated by lower drives. These values fail to lift people beyond themselves. Ultimate needs are sacrificed to meet immediate felt needs. It provides no basis to keep in check the negative side of the personality. As a result, the values communicated lead to destruction because there are no absolutes.

The fourth approach to values training may be described as "autonomous-directed." This approach is based on a specific view of individual personality development. This approach probably best represents the approach of contemporary American society. This approach is expressed in two ways, (1) the moral manager for efficiency and (2) the moral therapist for self-actualization.

The moral manager admires the self-made person. For those who take this approach, the motivation and strategy to attain is greater than the goal itself. The standard for managing life comes from the marketplace. Moral managers must manage resources and interpersonal relationships for calculated effectiveness. This results in dysfunctionalism as they divide the expectations and activities of life into compartments of work, home, recreation and religions. A person is a "winner" as he or she "takes control" of his or her life.

The moral therapist sees personal self-growth and actualization as the ultimate goal in any situation. He or she is willing to accept life's tensions arising from within the person and from the social, psychological, and technological demands of society. Life's focus is finding cures for growth and development. Solutions take the form of enhancement or empowerment to meet outer demands and inner desires. The standard for morality is a "specialist" who models resources for effective living or productivity. Morality and character is the liberation, development, and fulfillment of an individual.

In this approach to values training, authority rests in the process regardless of its end. Contemporary Boomers and Busters who work through the process become their own role models. Once again, this approach has its weakness. It provides no absolutes as a basis for morality. People are the center of their own morality. This approach offers no solutions to the problems of conflicting cultures and systems. Ultimately, it must oppose biblical morality to validate its existence.

HOW TO DEVELOP CHARACTER IN A HOSTILE CULTURE

Several generations ago, the values taught by parents to their children were reinforced by both the church and school. Society itself helped parents communicate Christian values to their children. That is no longer the case. The challenge facing us today personally and in ministry is that of developing godly character in a hostile culture. As we examine our paradigm for character development, there are six steps in building character in the next generation.

Character development begins with our thinking and understanding. Therefore, we must know God who is the source of our moral values. We must know the reasons and proof for our beliefs and how to apply His principles to life.

The next step in developing character involves our beliefs or assurance. This means we must make a total commitment to the demands of Scripture. Those who would have a godly character must yield their body, soul, and mind to Jesus Christ.

Step three involves our expectations and vision. We must realize God will give us power to overcome all things. Then, we should identify with those who will reinforce our biblical aspirations.

The next step deals with our values and attitudes. Identify the principles by which you live. Then challenge all negative values that creep into your life. Don't feed them and encourage their growth. Rather, reject their basic presuppositions.

The fifth step relates to our actions and life. Recognize the power that flows from right decisions. Do not wait for good feelings to do right. Instead, do right and you will feel good.

The final step in character development involves our accomplishments, i.e., the habits of our heart. If you do right, you will be right. Character is developed by practice, constantly practicing right. May God help you as you develop personal character and work to influence the character of the next generation.

Chapter 8:

BREAKING THE BONDAGE

ONE of the chief frustrations experienced by those wanting to break bad habits is an overwhelming inability to break free of the bondage associated with the habit. As much as they want to change, something inside refuses to let them take control. Sometimes, in the case of an addict, a physical addiction to some substance holds them in bondage. But even when no physical addiction is present, many people experience a psychological addiction to a habit that prevents them from making the significant change they long for.

These people are in bondage to habits they cannot break. They have tried unsuccessfully to free themselves, but have failed. Their problem is not a physical or mental one. They have a "besetting sin" that keeps them in bondage (Heb. 12:1). Their experience is not unique to this age. The apostle Paul lamented, "What I will to do, that I do not practice; but what I hate, that I do" (Rom. 7:15). He added, "for to will is present with me, but how to perform what is good I do not find" (Rom. 7:18).

For those of us who struggle with habits that have a grip on us that just won't let go, this chapter offers hope. The focus of this chapter is six steps that will help us break the cycle of sin and sinful habits that hold us in bondage.

Just as the process of forming habits begins with the way we think, so spiritual bondage has its roots in our mind. Most Christians would affirm their belief in God's omnipotence, yet many would also describe themselves as helpless victims unable to break the power of sin, our old nature, Satan, or a bad habit. There is a conflict between what we claim to believe and the bondage with which we struggle. This conflict is the result of believing Satan's lie.

Jesus warned the Jewish leaders of His day, "You are of your father the devil, and the desires of your father you want to do ... there is no truth in him. When he speaks a lie, he speaks from his own resources, for he is a liar and the father of it" (John 8:44). The mind is the center of control in our life. Whatever controls our mind has power over us. Satan attempts to gain control of our mind with the lie that our problems are bigger than God's ability to deal with them.

When we attempt to break a habit without taking into account the spiritual bondage associated with that habit, we will experience the frustration and discouragement that is characteristic of persistent failure. To break spiritual bondage, we must use the weapons God has provided for spiritual warfare. These "weapons of our warfare are not carnal but mighty in God for pulling down strongholds, casting down arguments and every high thing that exalts itself against the knowledge of God, bringing every thought into captivity to the obedience of Christ" (2 Cor. 10:4-5).

STEP ONE: COUNTERFEIT VERSUS REAL

The first step in breaking spiritual bondage involves discerning reality from that which is counterfeit. This involves recognizing and renouncing any control over your mind that is not Christ. "As the serpent deceived Eve by his craftiness, so your minds may be corrupted from the simplicity that is in Christ" (2 Cor. 11:3).

That which is counterfeit may come from one of several sources. The anti-Christian values learned in an ungodly home impact generations within the family. All of us have been exposed to the godless influence of the mass media in the books, movies, and music we experience. Have you ever been involved innocently or actively in the occult, new age, spiritism, black or white magic, cults, or other religions? These sources represent other sources of the counterfeit in our lives. Satanic rituals and bonding oneself to alien spirits also places people in spiritual bondage.

Jesus contrasted His ministry with that of the Devil when He stated, "The thief does not come except to steal, and to kill, and to destroy. I have come that they may have life, and that they may have it more abundantly" (John 10:10). In order to experience the abundant life Jesus promised and be free of spiritual bondage, we must renounce the counterfeit influences in our life. This involves praying audibly, "I renounce (insert here those counterfeit influences which are holding you in spiritual bondage)." This is the first important step on the road to experiencing your liberty in Christ.

STEP TWO: DECEPTION VERSUS TRUTH

The second step on the road to Christian liberty involves discerning truth from that which is deceptive. For many people, this step is very difficult. It involves our acknowledging our own efforts at deceiving ourselves and embracing God's truth in its place. God wants to begin the process of liberating us from spiritual bondage on the inside. David wrote, "Behold, You desire truth in the inward parts, and in the hidden part You will make me to know wisdom" (Psalm 51:6).

The problem with self-deception lies in the degree of success with which we achieve it. Many people have deceived themselves so long they have difficulty believing they are deceived. Several biblical principles may be applied to discern areas in which we have deceived ourselves. First, we deceive ourselves when we hear and fail to apply the Word of God in our life (James 1:22). Second, "if we say that we have no sin, we deceive ourselves, and the truth is not in us" (1 John 1:8). Also, "if anyone thinks himself to be something, when he is nothing, he deceives himself" (Gal. 6:3). A fourth way we deceive ourselves is to evaluate our wisdom by the standard of our age rather than the wisdom of God (1 Cor. 3:18). Finally, we deceive ourselves when we think we can sin and escape the consequences (1 Cor. 6:9).

As long as we continue to deceive ourselves, we will remain in spiritual bondage. In contrast, Jesus said, "You shall know the truth, and the truth shall make you free" (John 8:32). To move out of the realm of self-deception into the liberating truth of the Gospel, we must admit we are deceived. This involves praying audibly, "I admit (insert here those areas in which you have deceived yourself)." When we are honest with God and ourselves, we allow God's truth to free us from deception.

STEP THREE: BITTERNESS VERSUS FORGIVENESS

Step three on the path to liberty involves forgiving others to overcome bitterness and gain freedom. Refusing to forgive others results in spiritual bondage. Paul reminded the Corinthians, "Now whom you forgive anything, I also forgive. For if indeed I have forgiven anything, I have forgiven that one for your sakes in the presence of Christ, lest Satan should take advantage of us; for we are not ignorant of his devices" (2 Cor. 2:10-11).

As we work through this step, we need to make a list of the names of those we need to forgive. This is a list of names, not a list of sins or other violations which they may have committed against us or someone we are close to. Continually bringing up past sins is evidence that we have not forgiven them.

Forgiveness is a choice. Since God requires us to forgive others, it is something we *can* do. Our natural inclination is to seek revenge when we have suffered. But when we don't want to let others "off the hook," it means they still have their hooks in us. That places us in bondage to them. If we don't forgive others for their sakes, we should forgive them for our sakes.

When we deal with the issue of forgiveness, we are no longer considering a conflict between us and them, but a matter between us and God. When we forgive, we choose to live with the consequences of wrongs committed against us. If we do not forgive, we live with bitter consequences. The choice is ours.

We can choose whether to live in the freedom of forgiveness or in the bitterness of bondage. This involves praying audibly, "I forgive (insert here the names of those who have wronged you in some way)." As we forgive others, we experience God's forgiveness in our life.

STEP FOUR: REBELLION VERSUS SUBMISSION

The fourth step involves overcoming rebellion in our life by submitting to the authority of God and those He has placed over us. Jesus compared being under authority to a demonstration of great faith (Matt. 8:10). This involves trusting not only God directly, but also the line of authority He has appointed to provide leadership in our life God has placed all of us "under authority." We are called to submit to the authority of (1) civil government (Rom. 13:17), (2) church leadership (Heb. 13:17), (3) parents (Eph. 6:1-3), (4) husbands (1 Peter 3:1-4) (5) employers (1 Peter 2:1323), and (6) God (Dan. 9:5, 9) in the sphere of influence each of these has in our life. Dealing with a rebellious spirit or attitude and placing ourselves under authority involves praying audibly, "I submit to (insert here the specific authority in your life)." Submitting to these authorities God has placed in our life is an evidence of our submission to God Himself.

STEP FIVE: PRIDE VERSUS HUMILITY

Step five confronts the problem of pride with a spirit of humility. We must overcome bondage in our life through the freedom of Jesus Christ. When we sin habitually without self-control, we are in bondage. Jesus Christ wants you to be free. He promised, "Therefore if the Son makes you free, you shall be free indeed" (John 8:36). But what about our sins and failures?

Freedom is not being passive. We are free to actively do what we want to do. The key to experiencing full freedom in Christ is to take responsibility for our actions. When we confess our sins, God promises both cleansing and forgiveness (1 John 1:9). But how many times can you get forgiveness? Many Protestants suffer from a condition I call "confessionitis." This is the same "confession box" cycle of Roman Catholics. They confess their sins, but then immediately return to their sin after confession because they are in bondage.

The cure for confessionitis is found in the way we confess our sins. We should not just say, "I'm sorry for (insert specific sin here)." This leaves us with excuses for our actions like "I couldn't help it" or "The Devil made me do it." Instead, we should say, "I am responsible for (insert specific sin here)." We are responsible to not allow sin habitual control over our bodies (Rom. 6:13). We are called upon to renounce every sin done in our body by us or another. This involves praying audibly, "I take responsibility (insert specific sin here)." When this becomes the honest, prayer of our heart, we humble ourselves before God enabling Him to bless us with the freedom He desires to give us.

disown the sins of others and their influence on our life (Gal. 5:24; Ex. 20:4-5).

This may appear easier said than done. Actually, there are a few simple steps that can help us through this process. First, recognize you have been crucified, buried, and raised with Jesus Christ and you now sit in the heavenlies (2 Cor. 4:14). Second, publicly state you belong to the Lord Jesus Christ (Gal. 5:24). Then verbally claim the blood of Jesus over the Evil One (1 Cor. 6:20; 1 John 1:7). This involves praying audibly, "I disown (insert specific negative influences in your life)." These steps can help you break the influence of things that might otherwise keep your family in bondage for generations to come.

These are challenging days in which to build godly character in our own life and in the lives of others in our sphere of influence. Regardless, God still calls His people to a lifestyle characterized by personal holiness (1 Peter 1:16). As you break free of spiritual bondage and strive to develop godly character, may God make you strong in character and may the habits of your heart bring glory to Jesus Christ.

STEP SIX: BONDAGE VERSUS FREEDOM

The final step to spiritual freedom involves renouncing the sinful influences that come by family and acquaintances. Each of us is predisposed to certain behavior by several sources including (1) inner despair, (2) genetics, (3) direct sinful stimulation, (4) wrong heroes, and (5) satanic or demonic activity. For many people, these things are part of their family heritage. To gain spiritual liberty over the bondage associated with these influences, we must

PART TWO

HABITS OF THE HEART

Lessons

HOW TO FORMULATE CHARACTER

A. INTRODUCTION: WHAT IS CHARACTER?

1. Model: To see **perfect character**, look at Jesus. "Christ lives in me, so I live in this earthly life by trusting in the Son of God" (Galatians 2:20, NLT).

2. Discipline: to be a useful Christian, **discipline** to be like Jesus. "I press on to possess that perfection for which Christ Jesus first possessed me" (Philippians 3:12, NLT).

3. Your overall process:

    a. What you believe (**content** of your faith).

    b. Process by which you believe (**foundation**).

    c. How you live daily (**actions/habits**).

    d. Who you are, your (**character**).

4. Peter describes your daily process. "God has given us powerful yet precious promises ... break your old lust and transform yourself daily to be followers of Christ ... by adding faith to your **knowledge** of Scriptures, then add virtue (**life's vision**), next self-control (**disciple**), also add patient actions (**daily**), and finally your life (**character**) will live for God, becoming kind, and loving. When these increase you will keep from being ineffective and unproductive"" (2 Peter 1:4-8, ELT).

B. SIX STEPS TO CHANGE YOUR CHARACTER

1. Change your thinking to change your **belief**.

   a. Belief must be more than a mental decision, belief must be a commitment to a **life** of discipleship.

   b. Commitment to belief because it is **true**.

2. Change your belief to change your **expectations**.

   a. Some never see.

   b. Others see but not understand.

   c. Others see but never pursue.

   d. Others see but never feel.

   e. Others see and with obedience achieve it.

   f. Others see the vision and shares it to get others to purse it with them.

3. Change your expectations to change your **attitude**.

   a. Attitude is your **predisposition** to life.

   b. Can be defined/described as a **habit**.

   c. A predisposition/habit can be described as your **character**.

FOUR STEPS TO DEVELOP NEW ATTITUDE/HABIT

- **<u>Identify</u>** your problem.

- Identify right thinking that will **<u>change you</u>**.

- Relate/identify with positive people

- Develop/implement plan/thinking for positive attitude.

1. Change your attitude, change your **<u>actions</u>**.

    a. Your actions reflect your reputation.

    b. "Even a child is known by his deeds, whether he does what is pure and right" (Proverbs 20:11). Jesus said, "a tree is known by its own fruit" (Luke 6:44).

2. Change your actions, change your habits. Habits, "defines your position, i.e., your continual **<u>thinking and actions</u>**, i.e., "accomplished pianist."

3. Change your habits, change your character. First, we **<u>think</u>** it, we know it, we **<u>dream</u>** it, we focus on it, we **<u>act</u>** on it, that leads to **<u>accomplishment</u>**.

Lesson 1

HOW TO FORMULATE CHARACTER

A. INTRODUCTION: WHAT IS CHARACTER?

1. Model: To see _____ , look at Jesus. "Christ lives in me, so I live in this earthly life by trusting in the Son of God" (Galatians 2:20, NLT).

2. Discipline: to be a useful Christian, _____ to be like Jesus. "I press on to possess that perfection for which Christ Jesus first possessed me" (Philippians 3:12, NLT).

3. Your overall process:

   a. What you believe (_____ of your faith).

   b. Process by which you believe (_____).

   c. How you live daily (_____).

   d. Who you are, your (_____).

Peter describes your daily process. "God has given us powerful yet precious promises ... break your old lust and transform yourself daily to be followers of Christ ... by adding faith to your _____ of Scriptures, then add virtue (_____), next self-control (_____), also add patient actions (_____), and finally your life (_____) will live for God, becoming kind, and loving. When these increase you will keep from being ineffective and unproductive"" (2 Peter 1:4-8, ELT).

B. SIX STEPS TO
CHANGE YOUR CHARACTER

1. Change your thinking to change your _____ .

    a. Belief must be more than a mental decision, belief must be a commitment to a _____ of discipleship.

    b. Commitment to belief because it is _____ .

2. Change your belief to change your _____ .

    a. Some never see.

    b. Others see but not understand.

    c. Others see but never pursue.

    d. Others see but never feel.

    e. Others see and with obedience achieve it.

    f. Others see the vision and shares it to get others to purse it with them.

3. Change your expectations to change your _____ .

    a. Attitude is your _____ to life.

    b. Can be defined/described as a _____ .

    c. A predisposition/habit can be described as your _____ .

FOUR STEPS TO
DEVELOP NEW ATTITUDE/HABIT

- _____ your problem.

- Identify right thinking that will _____ .

- Relate/identify with positive people

- Develop/implement plan/thinking for positive attitude.

1. Change your attitude, change your _____ .

    a. Your actions reflect your reputation.

    b. "Even a child is known by his deeds, whether he does what is pure and right" (Proverbs 20:11). Jesus said, "a tree is known by its own fruit" (Luke 6:44).

2. Change your actions, change your habits. Habits, "defines your position, i.e., your continual _____ , i.e., "accomplished pianist."

Change your habits, change your character. First, we _____ it, we know it, we _____ it, we focus on it, we _____ on it, that leads to _____ .

Lesson 2

TOTAL LIFE DEVELOPMENT

A. INTRODUCTION

1. Just as a person getting ready to run a marathon, they must make a mental and emotional decision to get physically fit for the event. So, the development of character means total life development.

2. Belief System Cycle: **Formation of Character**:

   Thinking/<u>Understanding</u> – Belief/<u>Conviction</u> – Expectations/<u>Vision</u> – Attitudes/<u>Values</u> – Actions/<u>Life</u> – Accomplishments/<u>Habits</u> – **CHARACTER**

3. What is the most ridiculous argument for smoking that you have heard?

   c. It is all right to smoke because Rebekah "lighted off the camel" (Genesis 24:64).

   d. God approved smoking. "A smoking flax shall he not quench" (Isaiah 42:3).

B. CHARACTER MUST BE GROUNDED ON GOD'S PLAN

Believers must study the Bible to determine the principles by which they live.

1. How to discern biblical principles which develop character.

   a. Follow the clear **command** of Scriptures (Ephesians 6:1).

   b. Avoid a clear **negation** of Scriptures (Ephesians 4:31).

   c. Avoid circumstances that will **harm** your Christian life (1 Corinthians 6:14).

   d. Be committed to a pure **through life** (Matthew 5:28).

   e. Do not be a **stumbling block** for others (1 Corinthians 8:9).

   f. Obey your **conscience**, do not violate it (James 4:17).

   g. Do not intentionally harm your **body** (1 Corinthians 6:18-19).

   h. Do not do anything that cannot be carried out in **faith** (Romans 14:23).

2. How to determine biblical principles.

   a. Must be trans **cultural** (Matthew 10:5).

   b. Must be trans **temporal** (Romans 13:1, 4).

   c. Look **beyond** the actual to the principle (Matthew 5:41).

C. CHARACTER MUST BE GROUNDED ON THINKING/UNDERSTANDING

1. How to think about the Bible.

   a. Think with a **yielded** spirit.

   b. Ask the **Holy Spirit** to teach you (John 14:6).

   c. Think **practically**. Ask how you can apply this principle to your life.

   d. Think **holy**. Ask how you can become like God.

2. How to interpret the Bible.

   a. The golden rule of interpretation: "When the plain sense of Scriptures makes common sense, seek no other sense, but take every word at it's primary literal meaning." ~ David Cooper

   b. In light of the **historical context** – background.

   c. In light of the **author's original** plan and purpose.

   d. In light of the **context** (2 Peter 1:20).

   e. In light of the author's **meaning** of words.

D. PRINCIPLES TO GROW CHARACTER

1. The **Love** Principle. When properly motivated by love, you respect people and the law. You do right because you love others.

2. The **Loyalty** Principle. Because you have yielded to Christ, you do right to please Him.

3. The **Education** Principle. You do right because of what you have learned.

4. The **Training** Principle. You do right because you have done right so many times that it is a way of life with you.

5. The **Reward** Principle. You do right because of the satisfaction it gives.

6. The **Punishment** Principle. You do right because of the consequences you will get from doing wrong.

7. The **Fear** Principle. You do right because of unsettling emotions when you do wrong.

Lesson 2

TOTAL LIFE DEVELOPMENT

A. INTRODUCTION

1. Just as a person getting ready to run a marathon, they must make a mental and emotional decision to get physically fit for the event. So, the development of character means total life development.

2. Belief System Cycle: **Formation of Character**:

Thinking/ _____ – Belief/ _____ – Expectations/ _____ –
Attitudes/ _____ – Actions/ _____ –
Accomplishments/ _____ – **CHARACTER**

3. What is the most ridiculous argument for smoking that you have heard?

    a. It is all right to smoke because Rebekah "lighted off the camel" (Genesis 24:64).

    b. God approved smoking. "A smoking flax shall he not quench" (Isaiah 42:3).

B. CHARACTER MUST BE GROUNDED ON GOD'S PLAN

Believers must study the Bible to determine the principles by which they live.

1. How to discern biblical principles which develop character.

    a. Follow the clear _____ of Scriptures (Ephesians 6:1).

    b. Avoid a clear _____ of Scriptures (Ephesians 4:31).

    c. Avoid circumstances that will _____ your Christian life (1 Corinthians 6:14).

    d. Be committed to a pure _____ (Matthew 5:28).

    e. Do not be a _____ for others (1 Corinthians 8:9).

    f. Obey your _____ , do not violate it (James 4:17).

    g. Do not intentionally harm your _____ (1 Corinthians 6:18-19).

    h. Do not do anything that cannot be carried out in _____ (Romans 14:23).

2. How to determine biblical principles.

    a. Must be trans _____ (Matthew 10:5).

    b. Must be trans _____ (Romans 13:1, 4).

    c. Look _____ the actual to the principle (Matthew 5:41).

C. CHARACTER MUST BE GROUNDED ON THINKING/UNDERSTANDING

1. How to think about the Bible.

    a. Think with a _____ spirit.

    b. Ask the _____ to teach you (John 14:6).

    c. Think _____ . Ask how you can apply this principle to your life.

    d. Think _____ . Ask how you can become like God.

2. How to interpret the Bible.

   a. The golden rule of interpretation: "When the plain sense of Scriptures makes common sense, seek no other sense, but take every word at it's primary literal meaning." ~ David Cooper

   b. In light of the _____ – background.

   c. In light of the _____ plan and purpose.

   d. In light of the _____ (2 Peter 1:20).

   e. In light of the author's _____ of words.

D. PRINCIPLES TO GROW CHARACTER

1. The _____ Principle. When properly motivated by love, you respect people and the law. You do right because you love others.

2. The _____ Principle. Because you have yielded to Christ, you do right to please Him.

3. The _____ Principle. You do right because of what you have learned.

4. The _____ Principle. You do right because you have done right so many times that it is a way of life with you.

5. The _____ Principle. You do right because of the satisfaction it gives.

6. The _____ Principle. You do right because of the consequences you will get from doing wrong.

7. The _____ Principle. You do right because of unsettling emotions when you do wrong.

Lesson 3

ATTITUDE ADJUSTMENTS

A. INTRODUCTION

1. The development of character will become the basis for success in all you do.

2. The person with character has learned to constantly do the right thing with the right attitude for the right purpose.

3. Belief System Cycle: **Formation of Character**

   Belief/**Conviction** – Expectations/**Vision** – Attitudes/**Values** – Actions/**Life** – Accomplishments/**Habits** – Thinking/**Understanding** -- **CHARACTER**

4. Wrong attitudes lead to weak character.
   a. It's not my **responsibility**.
   b. No one will **see me** do it.
   c. No one **cares** if I do it.
   d. Everyone else is **doing it**.

B. PROPER ATTITUDES DEVELOP CHARACTER

1. Study influences. Who has greatly influenced you?

2. What makes a person successful in work? Carnegie Institute found 15% **skills** and 85% **personality**. Your personality is formed by attitudes and grows out of your character.

3. Why is a person fired? **30%** incompetence, **53%** personality, **27%** other reasons.

4. You cannot determine your circumstances, but when you have the right attitude you get the best out of circumstances and rise above circumstances. Why me? Why this? Why now?

5. You cannot determine your emotional response, but when you have the right attitude, you can rise above your feelings. You cannot **stop** feelings, but you can keep your feelings from **stopping** you.

C. BAD ATTITUDES WILL KEEP YOU FROM CONTINUOUS SUCCESS

1. Wrong attitudes do five things to you.

    a. Sours your **confidence**.

    b. Misdirects your **efforts**.

    c. Dilutes your **stamina** and purpose.

    d. Jams your **planning**.

    e. Cuts you off from **help**.

2. If you think you are beaten, you are. If you think you dare not, you don't. If you would like to win, but think you cannot, it is almost certain you won't.

D. WE ARE RESPONSIBLE FOR OUR ATTITUDES

1. Don't give excuses.

    a. Marriage failed because **married wrong**.

    b. Job stagnate because **don't like it**.

    c. School goes bad because **hate it**.

2. Your lousy **attitude** is an option. You can change.

3. The pessimist **complains** about the wind. The optimist **expects** a better wind. The person with **character** changes the sail.

4. God tells you to take control of your attitude. "Constantly remind the people about these laws, and you yourself must **think** about them every day and every night so that you will be sure to **obey** all of them. For only then will you succeed. Yes, be **bold** and strong! Banish fear and **doubt**! For remember, the Lord your God is with you wherever you go." (Joshua 1:8-9, TLB).

5. Motivation to do good.

   a. **Extrinsic** – outward motivation

   b. **Intrinsic** – inward motivation

   c. **Christocentric** – "For me to live it Christ" (Philippians 1:21). Also see Philippines 4:13.

E. WE MUST CHOOSE GOOD ATTITUDES

1. "Life is a choice." —John Maxwell

2. God chooses **what** you will go thorough, you choose **how** you will go through it.

3. "Every time you make a choice, you are turning the control part of you into something a little different from what it was before. And taking your life as a whole, with all its innumerable choices, you are slowly turning the control thing either into a heavenly creature or into a hellish one." —C. S. Lewis

4. We can determine our strength of the following: **faith**, love, **joy**, peace, humility, kindness, and **self-discipline**.

Lesson 3

QUESTIONS

ATTITUDE ADJUSTMENTS

A. INTRODUCTION

1. The development of character will become the basis for success in all you do.

2. The person with character has learned to constantly do the right thing with the right attitude for the right purpose.

3. Belief System Cycle: **Formation of Character**

    Belief/ _____ – Expectations/ _____ – Attitudes/ _____
    – Actions/ _____ – Accomplishments/ _____ –
    Thinking/ _____ – **CHARACTER**

4. Wrong attitudes lead to weak character.

    a. It's not my _____ .

    b. No one will _____ do it.

    c. No one _____ if I do it.

    d. Everyone else is _____ .

B. PROPER ATTITUDES DEVELOP CHARACTER

1. Study influences. Who has greatly influenced you?

2. What makes a person successful in work? Carnegie Institute found 15% _____ and 85% _____ . Your personality is formed by attitudes and grows out of your character.

3. Why is a person fired? _____ incompetence, _____ personality, _____ other reasons.

4. You cannot determine your circumstances, but when you have the right attitude you get the best out of circumstances and rise above circumstances.   me? Why this? Why now?

5. You cannot determine your emotional response, but when you have the right attitude, you can rise above your feelings. You cannot _____ feelings, but you can keep your feelings from _____ you.

C. BAD ATTITUDES WILL KEEP YOU FROM CONTINUOUS SUCCESS

1. Wrong attitudes do five things to you.

   a. Sours your _____ .

   b. Misdirects your _____ .

   c. Dilutes your _____ and purpose.

   d. Jams your _____ .

   e. Cuts you off from _____ .

2. If you think you are beaten, you are. If you think you dare not, you don't. If you would like to win, but think you cannot, it is almost certain you won't.

D. WE ARE RESPONSIBLE FOR OUR ATTITUDES

1. Don't give excuses.

   a. Marriage failed because _____ .

   b. Job stagnate because _____ .

   c. School goes bad because _____ .

2. Your lousy _____ is an option. You can change.

3. The pessimist _____ about the wind. The optimist _____ a better wind. The person with _____ changes the sail.

4. God tells you to take control of your attitude. "Constantly remind the people about these laws, and you yourself must _____ about them every day and every night so that you will be sure to _____ all of them. For only then will you succeed. Yes, be _____ and strong! Banish fear and _____ ! For remember, the Lord your God is with you wherever you go." (Joshua 1:8-9, TLB).

5. Motivation to do good.

    a. _____ – outward motivation

    b. _____ – inward motivation

    c. _____ – "For me to live it Christ" (Philippians 1:21). Also see Philippines 4:13.

E. WE MUST CHOOSE GOOD ATTITUDES

1. "Life is a choice." —John Maxwell

2. God chooses _____ you will go thorough, you choose _____ you will go through it.

3. "Every time you make a choice, you are turning the control part of you into something a little different from what it was before. And taking your life as a whole, with all its innumerable choices, you are slowly turning the control thing either into a heavenly creature or into a hellish one." —C. S. Lewis

4. We can determine our strength of the following: _____ , love, _____ , peace, humility, kindness, and _____ .

BASIS FOR SUCCESS IN CHRISTIAN LIFE AND SERVICE

A. INTRODUCTION

1. Development of **biblical character** is the basis for success in your Christian life and service.

2. What is Character?

    a. Webster: "Moral excellence and firmness."

    b. Oxford: "Moral constitution."

    c. Towns: "Moral character is your **predisposition** to right attitudes and right actions based on right reasons."

    d. The **focus** of your actions. The **habit** that guides your behavior. The controlling **values** of your personality.

3. What comes first, good **character** or good **behavior**?

4. Which of the following is based on **biblical** character?

    a. Doing right because I have never done wrong.

    b. Doing right because I am ignorant of wrong.

    c. Doing right because I am afraid I will get caught.

    d. Doing right because I will get rewards.

    e. Doing right because my friends do right.

5. The person with character has learned to consistently do the right **thing** with the right **attitude** for the right **purpose**.

B. THE BELIEF SYSTEM CYCLE: FORMATION OF CHARACTER

Belief/**Conviction** – Expectations/**Vision** – Attitudes/**Values** – Actions/**Life** – Accomplishments/**Habits** – Thinking/**Understanding** -- **CHARACTER**

C. COMPARISON OF RIGHT AND LEFT PERSONS

1. The person with character has the ability to carry out a decision long after the emotions are gone that influenced the choice.

2. Left-sided people:

   a. **Emotion** based.

   b. What is **easiest**?

   c. When I feel good then I will **do** it.

   d. Controlled by **moods**.

   e. **Selfish** mind-set.

   f. Life and lips **disagree**.

   g. Looks for **excuses**.

   h. **Outwardly** influenced.

   i. **Quits** during tough times.

   j. This person **whines**.

3. Right-sided people:

    a. **Character** based.

    b. What is **right**.

    c. When I do it, then I will **feel** good.

    d. Controlled by **priorities**.

    e. **Servanthood** mind-set.

    f. Life and lips **agree**.

    g. Looks for **solutions**.

    h. **Inwardly** influenced.

    i. **Continue** during tough times.

    j. This person **wins**.

4. "Right-sided people will have **long-lasting** friendships, **successful** marriages, **satisfying** vocations, and an **inward** happiness." —John Maxwell

D. HOW TO STEP FROM THE LEFT TO THE RIGHT SIDE

1. Power of decisions. Make a **commitment** to develop character (Luke 9:23).

2. Do right till the stars fall. Focus on **right reasons** for all you do (Matthew 6:33).

3. You can do what you want to do. Establish a habit of doing things that are **right** (Colossians 3:23).

4. Become **other person** focused (Matthew 5:46).

5. Be firm in your commitment, but be **patient and flexible** with your inability to do all you desire (Jeremiah 1:6-7).

6. **Verbalize** your principles so that you remember your expectations and how to apply them (Habakkuk 2:2).

7. **Track record**. When confronted with the problems and decisions of life:

    a. Look first to your **principles**.

    b. Gather all the **facts** you can.

    c. Apply workable **solutions**, (Philippians 3:13-14).

8. Your success will give you confidence and build **character** (Philippians 4:13).

Lesson 4

BASIS FOR SUCCESS IN CHRISTIAN LIFE AND SERVICE

A. INTRODUCTION

1. Development of _____ is the basis for success in your Christian life and service.

2. What is Character?

    a. Webster: "Moral excellence and firmness."

    b. Oxford: "Moral constitution."

    c. Towns: "Moral character is your _____ to right attitudes and right actions based on right reasons."

    d. The _____ of your actions. The _____ that guides your behavior. The controlling _____ of your personality.

3. What comes first, good _____ or good _____ ?

4. Which of the following is based on _____ character?

    a. Doing right because I have never done wrong.

    b. Doing right because I am ignorant of wrong.

    c. Doing right because I am afraid I will get caught.

    d. Doing right because I will get rewards.

    e. Doing right because my friends do right.

5. The person with character has learned to consistently do the right _____ with the right _____ for the right _____ .

B. THE BELIEF SYSTEM CYCLE: FORMATION OF CHARACTER

Belief/ _____ – Expectations/ _____ –
Attitudes/ _____ – Actions/ _____ –
Accomplishments/ _____ – Thinking/ _____ – **CHARACTER**

C. COMPARISON OF RIGHT AND LEFT PERSONS

1. The person with character has the ability to carry out a decision long after the emotions are gone that influenced the choice.

2. Left-sided people:

   a. _____ based.

   b. What is _____ ?

   c. When I feel good then I will _____ it.

   d. Controlled by _____ **s**.

   e. _____ mind-set.

   f. Life and lips _____ .

   g. Looks for _____ .

   h. _____ influenced.

   i. _____ during tough times.

   j. This person _____ .

3. Right-sided people:

    a. _____ based.

    b. What is _____ .

    c. When I do it, then I will _____ good.

    d. Controlled by _____ .

    e. _____ mind-set.

    f. Life and lips _____ .

    g. Looks for _____ .

    h. _____ influenced.

    i. _____ during tough times.

    j. This person _____ .

4. "Right-sided people will have _____ friendships, _____ marriages, _____ vocations, and an _____ happiness." —John Maxwell

D. HOW TO STEP FROM THE LEFT TO THE RIGHT SIDE

1. Power of decisions. Make a _____ to develop character (Luke 9:23).

2. Do right till the stars fall. Focus on _____ for all you do (Matthew 6:33).

3. You can do what you want to do. Establish a habit of doing things that are _____ (Colossians 3:23).

4. Become _____ focused (Matthew 5:46).

5. Be firm in your commitment, but be _____ with your inability to do all you desire (Jeremiah 1:6-7).

6. _____ your principles so that you remember your expectations and how to apply them (Habakkuk 2:2).

7. _____ . When confronted with the problems and decisions of life:

    a. Look first to your _____ **s**.

    b. Gather all the _____ you can.

    c. Apply workable _____ , (Philippians 3:13-14).

8. Your success will give you confidence and build _____ (Philippians 4:13).

Lesson 5

DEALING WITH CHANGE
AND GROWTH

A. INTRODUCTION

1. Does character come naturally, or do you have to make changes to get character? When you grow, you change. When you grow in character, you make decisions based on what you know, and it affects your feelings. You cannot grow without change, but you can change without growth. Growth is **change toward a goal**.

2. Observations of people with character:

   a. Everyone wants to change for the **better**.

   b. Everyone admires a person who had **changed for the better**.

   c. Very few people **change** for the better.

Formation of Character

Thinking/**Understanding** – Belief/**Conviction** – Expectation/**Vision** – Attitudes/**Values** – Actions/**Life** – Accomplishments/**Habits** – **CHARACTER**

3. Wrong approaches to growth or change:

   a. You ask God to change a **habit**.

   b. You ask God to change your **circumstances**.

   c. You ask God to change people **around** you. RIGHT APPROACH: Ask God to change **your approach** to life.

4. Wrong things to change:

   a. You change your action without changing your thinking **legalism**.

   b. You change once without permanent adjustments **experiments**.

   c. You change outward without inward **cosmetic**.

   d. You keep changing your thinking **confusion**. You change your fruit without changing the root **outward**.

B. PEOPLE WITH CHARACTER

1. Desire personal growth and development (Philippians 3:10).

2. Know how to grow and change (Philippians 3:13, 4:9), and have a strategy for growth and change.

3. Eliminate burdens and barriers (Hebrews 12:1).

   a. **Negative**. Get rid of distractions, weights, and hindrances.

   b. **Positive**. Become focused in your life.

4. Know how to overcome failure. Failure does not destroy you, your attitude toward failure stops you. We all have outward problems and disappointments within, but those with the **will** to **win** can overcome failure.

   a. There is a difference between "I failed" and "I am a failure." Don't war failure like a suit.

   b. Failure is **part of the journey** (1 Timothy 1:15).

   c. Don't let your failures **control** you.

   d. Learn something from every failure.

   e. Take responsibility, don't make **excuses**.

5. Have a dream/vision.

    a. Develop together. Does the person with vision go after character, or does the person with principles gravitate to purpose in life? What comes first?

    b. Character without vision **examples**.

    c. Vision without character **productive**.

    d. Both character and vision multiply **effectiveness**.

    e. **Live** outside yourself. People with character live by principles outside themselves. People with vision are motivated to goals outside themselves.

    f. Applied **action**. When you have a vision, it moves you to actualize its potential. When vision grows out of character, the person sees exactly how to make it happen and has the power and principles to make it happen.

DEALING WITH CHANGE AND GROWTH

A. INTRODUCTION

1. Does character come naturally, or do you have to make changes to get character? When you grow, you change. When you grow in character, you make decisions based on what you know, and it affects your feelings. You cannot grow without change, but you can change without growth. Growth is _____ .

2. Observations of people with character:

   a. Everyone wants to change for the _____ .

   b. Everyone admires a person who had _____ .

   c. Very few people _____ for the better.

Formation of Character

Thinking/ _____ – Belief/ _____ –
Expectation/ _____ – Attitudes/ _____ –
Actions/ _____ – Accomplishments/ _____ – **CHARACTER**

3. Wrong approaches to growth or change:

   a. You ask God to change a _____ .

   b. You ask God to change your _____ .

   c. You ask God to change people _____ you. RIGHT APPROACH: Ask God to change _____ to life.

4. Wrong things to change:

   a. You change your action without changing your thinking _____ .

   b. You change once without permanent adjustments _____ .

   c. You change outward without inward _____ .

   d. You keep changing your thinking _____ . You change your fruit without changing the root _____ .

B. PEOPLE WITH CHARACTER

1. Desire personal growth and development (Philippians 3:10).

2. Know how to grow and change (Philippians 3:13, 4:9), and have a strategy for growth and change.

3. Eliminate burdens and barriers (Hebrews 12:1).

   a. _____ . Get rid of distractions, weights, and hindrances.

   b. _____ . Become focused in your life.

4. Know how to overcome failure. Failure does not destroy you, your attitude toward failure stops you. We all have outward problems and disappointments within, but those with the _____ to _____ can overcome failure.

   a. There is a difference between "I failed" and "I am a failure." Don't war failure like a suit.

   b. Failure is _____ (1 Timothy 1:15).

   c. Don't let your failures _____ you.

   d. Learn something from every failure.

   e. Take responsibility, don't make _____ .

5. Have a dream/vision.

   a. Develop together. Does the person with vision go after character, or does the person with principles gravitate to purpose in life? What comes first?

   b. Character without vision _____ .

   c. Vision without character _____ .

   d. Both character and vision multiply _____ .

   e. _____ outside yourself. People with character live by principles outside themselves. People with vision are motivated to goals outside themselves.

   f. Applied _____ . When you have a vision, it moves you to actualize its potential. When vision grows out of character, the person sees exactly how to make it happen and has the power and principles to make it happen.

HABITS OF THE HEART

A. INTRODUCTION

1. The phrase, *Habits of the Heart*, was Tocqueville's description of America's virtue, character and morals.

2. Definition of habit: "A behavior pattern acquired by frequent repetition that is reflected in regular or increased performance."

3. Root: comes from root meaning clothing that is usually worn, i.e., a nun's habit.

4. No none is without habits, **good** and **bad** habits.

5. Habits are **voluntary** and **involuntary**.

6. Habits extend to every part of life:

    a. **Language** habits – thank you, cursing.

    b. **Emotional** habits – laughter, roll eyes.

    c. **Physical** habits – hand over cough, burp.

    d. **Instinctive** habits – drive car, stutter.

7. "If you do right, you will be right" Erin Towns, mother of Elmer Towns.

B. HOW WE RESPOND: A HABIT IS A WAY OF RESPONDING THAT HAS BEEN LEARNED

1. We think about the world:

   a. **Remember**. The ability to recreate the past and relate it to the present.

   b. **Anticipate**. The ability to predict a response or situation that will occur in the future.

   c. **Imagine**. The ability to conceive responses or situations that is not yet related to the present.

2. We perceive the world:

   a. To **receive** data. We can receive and understand information.

   b. To **interpret** data. We can give meaning to it and classify it with other information.

   c. To **respond** to data. We can respond properly to information. "The cat that sits on a hot stove, the cat will never sit on another hot stove, nor will the cat **sit on a cold stove**."

3. We fell about the world:

   a. **Emotions** are the response of your bodily state to a situation, anger, fear, alienation, depression.

   b. **Feelings** are the expression of the bodily state, happiness, strain, pressure, excitement.

C. DO WE BREAK HABITS OR MAKE HABITS?

1. A habit is formed by mere repetition: **True** or False

2. There is no such thing as a new habit, only the modification of old habits: True or **False**

3. Can we unlearn old habits by deliberate repetition to disintegrate the old? **True** or False

D. HOW TO BREAK OLD HABITS

1. **Know**. Understand your situation and condition in life (Romans 7:18).

2. **Look** at self. Be aware of your actual weakness (Romans 7:19).

3. **Evaluate**. Measure the intensity of negative influence that your inadequacy contributes to your life (Romans 7:24).

4. **Visualize**. Form an image of ideal behavior that you desire (Romans 6:14).

5. **Positionize**. See the result will come to you for eliminating negative habits (Romans 8:2).

6. **Want**. Create and feel a desire to realize these ideals (Romans 6:11).

7. **Reach**. Look outside yourself for vision, strength, and help (1 Thessalonians 5:23).

8. **Choice**. Make a decision.

9. **Act**. Engage persistently in the desired response (1 Thessalonians 5:21).

10. **Faith**. Trust God to complete the action you have begun (1 Thessalonians 5:24).

Lesson 6

HABITS OF THE HEART

A. INTRODUCTION

1. The phrase, *Habits of the Heart*, was Tocqueville's description of America's virtue, character and morals.

2. Definition of habit: "A behavior pattern acquired by frequent repetition that is reflected in regular or increased performance."

3. Root: comes from root meaning clothing that is usually worn, i.e., a nun's habit.

4. No none is without habits, _____ and _____ habits.

5. Habits are _____ and _____ .

6. Habits extend to every part of life:

   a. _____ habits – thank you, cursing.

   b. _____ habits – laughter, roll eyes.

   c. _____ habits – hand over cough, burp.

   d. _____ habits – drive car, stutter.

7. "If you do right, you will be right" Erin Towns, mother of Elmer Towns.

B. HOW WE RESPOND: A HABIT IS A WAY OF RESPONDING THAT HAS BEEN LEARNED

1. We think about the world:

    a. _____ . The ability to recreate the past and relate it to the present.

    b. _____ . The ability to predict a response or situation that will occur in the future.

    c. _____ . The ability to conceive responses or situations that is not yet related to the present.

2. We perceive the world:

    a. To _____ data. We can receive and understand information.

    b. To _____ data. We can give meaning to it and classify it with other information.

    c. To _____ to data. We can respond properly to information. "The cat that sits on a hot stove, the cat will never sit on another hot stove, nor will the cat _____ ."

3. We fell about the world:

    a. _____ are the response of your bodily state to a situation, anger, fear, alienation, depression.

    b. _____ are the expression of the bodily state, happiness, strain, pressure, excitement.

C. DO WE BREAK HABITS OR MAKE HABITS?

1. A habit is formed by mere repetition: _____

2. There is no such thing as a new habit, only the modification of old habits: _____

3. Can we unlearn old habits by deliberate repetition to disintegrate the old? _____

D. HOW TO BREAK OLD HABITS

1. _____ . Understand your situation and condition in life (Romans 7:18).

2. _____ at self. Be aware of your actual weakness (Romans 7:19).

3. _____ . Measure the intensity of negative influence that your inadequacy contributes to your life (Romans 7:24).

4. _____ . Form an image of ideal behavior that you desire (Romans 6:14).

5. _____ . See the result will come to you for eliminating negative habits (Romans 8:2).

6. _____ . Create and feel a desire to realize these ideals (Romans 6:11).

7. _____ . Look outside yourself for vision, strength, and help (1 Thessalonians 5:23).

8. _____ . Make a decision.

9. _____ . Engage persistently in the desired response (1 Thessalonians 5:21).

10. _____ . Trust God to complete the action you have begun (1 Thessalonians 5:24).

VALUES AND MORALITY

A. INTRODUCTION

1. The book, *Why Johnny Cannot Tell Right From Wrong* by William Kilpatrick, is a Catholic layman who attacks cultural relativism saying that nondirected methods of moral education which urges students to make equally valid choices in the jungle of relativism has actually encouraged youth to experiment with drug, sex, and lawlessness.

2. **Values clarification** is essentially doing what you want to or like to do, not what you ought to do.

B. SOURCES OF EROSION IN AMERICAN MORALITY

1. **Changing culture.** Harvey Cox's book, The Secular City shows culture in six pictures:

   a. The **tribe**.

   b. The **town**.

   c. The **metropolitan**.

   d. The **megalopolis**.

   e. The switchboard, **communication**.

   f. The cloverleaf, **transportation**.

2. Conflicting values of new immigrants.

3. Public schools no longer a conduit of morality.

4. Making the Bible a **myth** rather than the source of **morality**.

5. Retreat of the church from effective **teaching** (*didache*) and **preaching** (the *Kerugma*).

C. FOUR SOURCES OF MORALITY/CHARACTER:

Suggested by David Reisman, The Lonely Crowd

1. Tradition-directed values. Represented by immigrants and transmitted through the family.

   a. Irish Catholic

   b. Scandinavian

   c. Oriental

   d. Hispanic

   e. African

   f. Others

Actions/**Habits** – Attitudes/**Values** – Expectations/**Aims** – Belief/**Acceptance** – Thinking/**Why** – CHARACTER

Authority: _____

Role Model: _____

Weakness:

   a. No outward biblical standard

   b. Conflict with traditional America

   c. Conflict with other ethnic groups because of no absolute standard.

   d. Not able to reproduce self when removed from its culture.

   e. Problems with differences in clothing, language, music, and other outward expressions.

2. Inner-Directed Values. Represented by traditional American values which are an amalgamation of biblical ethics, American "worth of the individual," and republicanism. These prizes: **justice** (do right), **success** (get ahead), and **freedom** (individualism).

Thinking/**Understanding** – Belief/**Conviction** – Expectations/**Vision** –
Attitudes/**Values** – Actions/**Life** –Accomplishments/**Habits** – CHARACTER

Authority: _____

Role Model: _____

Weakness:

   a. Expect all to live by their values (superiority).

   b. Outward conformity produces legalism.

   c. Conflicts with the negative side of human nature.

   d. Openness and acceptance of other values becomes the seeds of its destruction.

3. Non-Driven Values (stimulus-response). Responds to or conforms to the pressures of others. Give in to the lower urges of the personality.

   a. Those who **backslide** from #1 or #2.

   b. Those who drop out of culture.

   c. A blend of the others.

Basic Drives/**Lust** – Stimulus Res./**Want** – Need/Fulfill/**Good** –
Actions/**Reinforced** – Habits/**Accomplishments** – CHARACTER

Authority: _____

Role Model: _____

Weakness:

   a. Values are motivated by lower drives.

   b. Will not lift people beyond themselves.

   c. Ultimate needs are sacrificial to immediate needs.

   d. No basis to keep in check the negative side of the personality.

   e. Leads to destruction.

   f. No absolutes.

4. Autonomous-Directed Values. Expresses developing personality of the individual. This falls into two categories: the moral manager for efficiency and the moral therapist for self-actualization.

   a. The Moral Manager:

      i. Admires the self-made person.

      ii. The motivation and strategy to attain is greater than the goal.

      iii. The standard to manage life comes from the marketplace.

      iv. Must manage resources and interpersonal relationship for calculated effectiveness.

      v. Divide the expectations and activities of life into compartments of work, home, recreation, religions, etc. (dysfunctional).

      vi. The person is a sinner and takes control of their life.

   g. The Moral Therapist:

      i. Personal self-growth and actualization is the goal.

      ii. Accepts life's tensions arising from within the person and from the social, psychological and technological demands of society.

      iii. Life's focus is finding curses for growth and development.

      iv. Solutions take the form of enhancement or empowerment to meet outer demands and inner desires.

      v. The standard for morality is a specialist who models resources for effective living or productivity.

      vi. Morality and character are the liberation, development, and fulfillment of individual.

Need/**Desire To Develop** – Focus/**Attain Self-Actualization** –
Organizes/Administers/**Resources** – Controlled/**Action** –
Receives/**Worth** – CHARACTER

Authority: _____

Role Model: _____

Weakness:

   a. No absolutes in basis for morality.

   b. Man is the center of morality.

   c. No solutions with conflicting cultures and systems.

   d. Must oppose biblical morality to validate its existence.

D. HOW TO DEVELOP CHARACTER IN A HOSTILE CULTURE

Thinking/Understanding:

1. Know **God**, who is the source of your morals.

2. Know the **reasons**, proof and how to apply your principles.

Beliefs/Assurance:

3. Make a total **commitment** to the demands of Scriptures.

4. Yield body, soul, and mind to Jesus Christ.

Expectations/Vision:

5. Realize God will give you **power** to overcome all things.

6. Identify with those who will reinforce your biblical aspirations.

Values/Attitudes:

7. Identify the **principles** by which you live.

8. Challenge all negative values that creep into your life. Don't feed them and reject their presupposition.

Actions/Life:

9. Recognize the power that flows from right decision.

10. Do not wait for good feeling to do right, do right and you will **feel good**.

Accomplishments/Habits:

11. If you do **right**, you will be **right** (character).

VALUES AND MORALITY

A. INTRODUCTION

1. The book, *Why Johnny Cannot Tell Right From Wrong* by William Kilpatrick, is a Catholic layman who attacks cultural relativism saying that nondirected methods of moral education which urges students to make equally valid choices in the jungle of relativism has actually encouraged youth to experiment with drug, sex, and lawlessness.

2. _____ is essentially doing what you want to or like to do, not what you ought to do.

B. SOURCES OF EROSION IN AMERICAN MORALITY

1. _____ . Harvey Cox's book, The Secular City shows culture in six pictures:

    a. The _____ .

    b. The _____ .

    c. The _____ .

    d. The _____ .

    e. The switchboard, _____ .

    f. The cloverleaf, _____ .

2. Conflicting values of new immigrants.

3. Public schools no longer a conduit of morality.

4. Making the Bible a _____ rather than the source of _____ .

5. Retreat of the church from effective _____ (*didache*) and _____ (the *Kerugma*).

C. FOUR SOURCES OF MORALITY/CHARACTER:

Suggested by David Reisman, The Lonely Crowd

1. Tradition-directed values. Represented by immigrants and transmitted through the family.

   a. Irish Catholic

   b. Scandinavian

   c. Oriental

   d. Hispanic

   e. African

   f. Others

Actions/ _____ – Attitudes/ _____ –
Expectations/ _____ – Belief/ _____ –
Thinking/ _____ – CHARACTER

Authority: _____

Role Model: _____

Weakness:

   a. No outward biblical standard

   b. Conflict with traditional America

   c. Conflict with other ethnic groups because of no absolute standard.

   d. Not able to reproduce self when removed from its culture.

   e. Problems with differences in clothing, language, music, and other outward expressions.

2. Inner-Directed Values. Represented by traditional American values which are an amalgamation of biblical ethics, American "worth of the individual," and republicanism. These prizes: _____ (do right), _____ (get ahead), and _____ (individualism).

Thinking/ _____ – Belief/ _____ –
Expectations/ _____ – Attitudes/ _____ –
Actions/ _____ –Accomplishments/ _____ – CHARACTER

Authority: _____

Role Model: _____

Weakness:

   a. Expect all to live by their values (superiority).

   b. Outward conformity produces legalism.

   c. Conflicts with the negative side of human nature.

   d. Openness and acceptance of other values becomes the seeds of its destruction.

3. Non-Driven Values (stimulus-response). Responds to or conforms to the pressures of others. Give in to the lower urges of the personality.

   a. Those who _____ from #1 or #2.

   b. Those who drop out of culture.

   c. A blend of the others.

Basic Drives/ _____ – Stimulus Res./ _____ –
Need/Fulfill/ _____ – Actions/ _____ –
Habits/ _____ – CHARACTER

Authority: _____

Role Model: _____

Weakness:

   a. Values are motivated by lower drives.

   b. Will not lift people beyond themselves.

   c. Ultimate needs are sacrificial to immediate needs.

   d. No basis to keep in check the negative side of the personality.

   e. Leads to destruction.

   f. No absolutes.

4. Autonomous-Directed Values. Expresses developing personality of the individual. This falls into two categories: the moral manager for efficiency and the moral therapist for self-actualization.

    a. The Moral Manager:

        i. Admires the self-made person.

        ii. The motivation and strategy to attain is greater than the goal.

        iii. The standard to manage life comes from the marketplace.

        iv. Must manage resources and interpersonal relationship for calculated effectiveness.

        v. Divide the expectations and activities of life into compartments of work, home, recreation, religions, etc. (dysfunctional).

        vi. The person is a sinner and takes control of their life.

    g. The Moral Therapist:

        i. Personal self-growth and actualization is the goal.

        ii. Accepts life's tensions arising from within the person and from the social, psychological and technological demands of society.

        iii. Life's focus is finding curses for growth and development.

        iv. Solutions take the form of enhancement or empowerment to meet outer demands and inner desires.

        v. The standard for morality is a specialist who models resources for effective living or productivity.

        vi. Morality and character are the liberation, development, and fulfillment of individual.

Need/ _____ – Focus/ _____ –
Organizes/Administers/ _____ – Controlled/ _____ –
Receives/ _____ – CHARACTER

Authority: _____

Role Model: _____

Weakness:

    a. No absolutes in basis for morality.

    b. Man is the center of morality.

    c. No solutions with conflicting cultures and systems.

    d. Must oppose biblical morality to validate its existence.

D. HOW TO DEVELOP CHARACTER IN A HOSTILE CULTURE

Thinking/Understanding:

1. Know _____ , who is the source of your morals.

2. Know the _____ , proof and how to apply your principles.

Beliefs/Assurance:

3. Make a total _____ to the demands of Scriptures.

4. Yield body, soul, and mind to Jesus Christ.

Expectations/Vision:

5. Realize God will give you _____ to overcome all things.

6. Identify with those who will reinforce your biblical aspirations.

Values/Attitudes:

7. Identify the _____ by which you live.

8. Challenge all negative values that creep into your life. Don't feed them and reject their presupposition.

Actions/Life:

9. Recognize the power that flows from right decision.

10. Do not wait for good feeling to do right, do right and you will _____ .

Accomplishments/Habits:

11. If you do _____ , you will be _____ (character).

BREAKING BONDAGE

A. INTRODUCTION

Some people are in bondage to habits they cannot break. They have tried unsuccessfully to free themselves but have failed. Their problem is not a physical or mental one. They have a *besetting sin* that keeps them in bondage (Hebrews 12:1). This lesson gives steps to breaking the bondage of habits.

1. **Head knowledge**. You know God is all powerful.

2. **Helpless victim**. You cannot break the power of your nature, satan, habits, etc.

3. **Problem is lies**. Satan's power is in lying to you. "You are of your father the devil, and the desires of your father you want to do . . . for he is a liar" (John 8:44).

4. **Center of control**. Your mind controls your life. Whatever controls your mind has power over you. "For the weapons of our warfare are not carnal but mighty in God . . . casting down arguments and every high thing that exalts itself against the knowledge of God, bringing every thought into captivity to the obedience of Christ" (1 Corinthians 10:4-5).

B. SIX STEPS TO BREAKING THE CYCLE OF HABITS THAT HAVE YOU IN BONDAGE

1. You must **recognize** and **renounce** any control over your mind that is not Christ. "As the serpent deceived Eve by his craftiness, so your minds may be corrupted from the simplicity that is in Christ" (1 Corinthians 11:3).

   a. Anti-Christian or ungodly home, godless influence, alien bond.

   b. Were you involved innocently or actively in an occult, new age, spiritism, black or white magic, cults, or other religions?

   c. Satanic rituals.

   d. Pray, "I recognize..."

2. You must acknowledge any **self-deception** and embrace the truth of God.

   a. Recognizing freedom begins with the **mind** (Psalm 51:6).

   b. Recognize self-deception in: Hearing but not **doing** Scriptures, "deceiving your own selves" (James 1:22). Not admitting your **sin**, "We deceive ourselves" (1 John 1:8). Thinking we are **something**, "thinks himself" (Galatians 6:3). Thinking we are **smart**, "deceive himself" (1 Corinthians 3:18). By **sinning**, "be not deceived" (1 Corinthians 6:9).

   c. Pray, "I admit ..."

3. You must forgive others to overcome **bitterness** and get **freedom**.

   a. If you refuse to forgive, satan has an advantage over you (2 Corinthians 2:10-11).

   b. Make a list of their names, not their **sins**.

   c. When you continually bring up the past, you have not forgiven them.

   d. Forgiveness is a **choice**. Since God requires you to forgive, it is something you can you.

   e. You naturally want revenge because you suffered.

   f. When you don't want to let them off the **hook**, it means they still have their **hooks** in you. You are in bondage to them.

   g. You don't forgive them for **their sake**, you forgive them for **your sake**.

   h. The issue is no longer between **you and them**, but between **you and God**.

   i. When you forgive, you **choose** to live with their consequences. If you do not forgive, you still live with bitter consequences.

   j. You can choose whether to live in the **freedom of forgiveness** or the **bitterness of bondage**.

   k. Pray, "I forgive..."

4. You must overcome __rebellion__ in your life by submitting to the __authority__ of God and those over you.

   a. Being under authority is an act of __faith__. You trust God and His line of authority to lead your life.

   b. We are to __submit__ to: civil government (Romans 13:1-7); church leadership (Hebrews 13:17), parents (Ephesians 6:1-3); husband (1 Peter 3:1-4), employers (1 Peter 2:13-23); God (Daniel 9:5, 9).

   c. Pray, "I submit..."

5. You must overcome __bondage__ in your life through the freedom of Jesus Christ.

   a. To sin habitually without self-control is to be in __bondage__.

   b. Jesus Christ wants you to be free (John 8:36), but what about your sins and failures?

   c. Freedom is not being passive. You are free to do (active) what you want to do. The key is to take responsibility for your actions. You get two virtues when you confess, __cleansing and forgiveness__ (1 John 1:9).

   d. How many times can you get forgiveness? Many people suffer the "confession box" cycle of Roman Catholics. They go back to sin after confession because they are in bondage.

   e. Don't just say, "I am sorry for it" but say, "I am __responsible__ for it." Our responsibility is to not allow sin to habitually control our bodies (Romans 6:13).

   f. __Renounce__ every sin done to your body by you or another.

   g. Pray, "I take responsibility..."

6. You must renounce sinful influences that come by family and acquaintances.

   a. You are __predisposed__ by several sources:

      i. Inward despair.

      ii. Genetically.

      iii. Immoral atmosphere.

      iv. Wrong heroes.

      v. Direct sinful stimulation.

      vi. Satanic/demonic activity.

   b. __Disown__ the sins of others and their influences on your life (Galatians 5:24; Exodus 20:4-5).

   c. __Recognize__ you have been crucified, buried and raised with Jesus Christ and you now sit in the heavenlies (2 Corinthians 4:14).

   d. __Publicly__ state you belong to the Lord Jesus Christ (Galatians 5:24).

   e. __Verbally__ claim the blood of Jesus over the evil one (1 Corinthians 6:20; 1 John 1:7).

   f. Pray, "I renounce..."

Lesson 8

BREAKING BONDAGE

A. INTRODUCTION

Some people are in bondage to habits they cannot break. They have tried unsuccessfully to free themselves but have failed. Their problem is not a physical or mental one. They have a *besetting sin* that keeps them in bondage (Hebrews 12:1). This lesson gives steps to breaking the bondage of habits.

1. _____ . You know God is all powerful.

2. _____ . You cannot break the power of your nature, satan, habits, etc.

3. _____ . Satan's power is in lying to you. "You are of your father the devil, and the desires of your father you want to do...for he is a liar" (John 8:44).

4. _____ . Your mind controls your life. Whatever controls your mind has power over you. "For the weapons of our warfare are not carnal but mighty in God . . . casting down arguments and every high thing that exalts itself against the knowledge of God, bringing every thought into captivity to the obedience of Christ" (1 Corinthians 10:4-5).

B. SIX STEPS TO BREAKING THE CYCLE OF HABITS THAT HAVE YOU IN BONDAGE

1. You must _____ and _____ any control over your mind that is not Christ. "As the serpent deceived Eve by his craftiness, so your minds may be corrupted from the simplicity that is in Christ" (1 Corinthians 11:3).

   a. Anti-Christian or ungodly home, godless influence, alien bond.

   b. Were you involved innocently or actively in an occult, new age, spiritism, black or white magic, cults, or other religions?

   c. Satanic rituals.

   d. Pray, "I recognize..."

2. You must acknowledge any _____ and embrace the truth of God.

   a. Recognizing freedom begins with the _____ (Psalm 51:6).

   b. Recognize self-deception in: Hearing but not _____ Scriptures, "deceiving your own selves" (James 1:22). Not admitting your _____ , "We deceive ourselves" (1 John 1:8). Thinking we are _____ , "thinks himself" (Galatians 6:3). Thinking we are _____ t, "deceive himself" (1 Corinthians 3:18). By _____ , "be not deceived" (1 Corinthians 6:9).

   c. Pray, "I admit ..."

3. You must forgive others to overcome _____ and get _____ .

   a. If you refuse to forgive, satan has an advantage over you (2 Corinthians 2:10-11).

   b. Make a list of their names, not their _____ .

   c. When you continually bring up the past, you have not forgiven them.

   d. Forgiveness is a _____ . Since God requires you to forgive, it is something you can you.

   e. You naturally want revenge because you suffered.

   f. When you don't want to let them off the _____ , it means they still have their _____ in you. You are in bondage to them.

   g. You don't forgive them for _____ , you forgive them for _____ .

   h. The issue is no longer between _____ , but between _____ .

   i. When you forgive, you _____ to live with their consequences. If you do not forgive, you still live with bitter consequences.

j. You can choose whether to live in the _____ or the _____ .

k. Pray, "I forgive..."

4. You must overcome _____ in your life by submitting to the _____ of God and those over you.

   a. Being under authority is an act of _____ . You trust God and His line of authority to lead your life.

   b. We are to _____ to: civil government (Romans 13:1-7); church leadership (Hebrews 13:17), parents (Ephesians 6:1-3); husband (1 Peter 3:1-4), employers (1 Peter 2:13-23); God (Daniel 9:5, 9).

   c. Pray, "I submit..."

5. You must overcome _____ in your life through the freedom of Jesus Christ.

   a. To sin habitually without self-control is to be in _____ .

   b. Jesus Christ wants you to be free (John 8:36), but what about your sins and failures?

   c. Freedom is not being passive. You are free to do (active) what you want to do. The key is to take responsibility for your actions. You get two virtues when you confess, _____ (1 John 1:9).

   d. How many times can you get forgiveness? Many people suffer the "confession box" cycle of Roman Catholics. They go back to sin after confession because they are in bondage.

   e. Don't just say, "I am sorry for it" but say, "I am _____ for it." Our responsibility is to not allow sin to habitually control our bodies (Romans 6:13).

   f. _____ every sin done to your body by you or another.

   g. Pray, "I take responsibility..."

6. You must renounce sinful influences that come by family and acquaintances.

   a. You are _____ by several sources:

      i.   Inward despair.

      ii. Genetically.

      iii. Immoral atmosphere.

      iv. Wrong heroes.

      v.   Direct sinful stimulation.

      vi. Satanic/demonic activity.

   b. _____ the sins of others and their influences on your life (Galatians 5:24; Exodus 20:4-5).

c. _____ you have been crucified, buried and raised with Jesus Christ and you now sit in the heavenlies (2 Corinthians 4:14).

d. _____ state you belong to the Lord Jesus Christ (Galatians 5:24).

e. _____ claim the blood of Jesus over the evil one (1 Corinthians 6:20; 1 John 1:7).

f. Pray, "I renounce..."

PART THREE

HABITS OF THE HEART

POWER POINT GUIDE

Habits of the Heart

Slide 1 of 100

How To Formulate Character

Slide 2 of 100

A. INTRODUCTION: WHAT IS CHARACTER?

1. Model: To see perfect character, look at Jesus. "Christ lives in me, so I live in this earthly life by trusting in the Son of God" (Galatians 2:20, NLT).

1. Discipline: to be a useful Christian, I discipline to be like Jesus. "I press on to possess that perfection for which Christ Jesus first possessed me" (Philippians 3:12, NLT).

Slide 3 of 100

3. Your overall process:
   a. What you believe (content of your faith).
   b. Process by which you believe (foundation).
   c. How you live daily (actions/habits).
   d. Who you are, your (character).

4. Peter describes your daily process. "God has given us powerful yet precious promises ... break your old lust and transform yourself daily to be followers of Christ ... by adding faith to your knowledge of Scriptures, then add virtue (life's vision), next self-control (disciple), also add patient actions (daily), and finally your life (character) will live for God, becoming kind, and loving. When these increase you will keep from being ineffective and unproductive" (2 Peter 1:4-8, ELT).

Slide 4 of 100

B. SIX STEPS TO CHANGE YOUR CHARACTER

1. Change your thinking to change your belief.
   a. Belief must be more than a mental decision; belief must be a commitment to a life of discipleship.
   b. Commitment to belief because it is true.

Slide 5 of 100

2. Change your belief to change your expectations.
   a. Some never see.
   b. Others see but not understand.
   c. Others see but never pursue.
   d. Others see but never feel.
   e. Others see and with obedience achieve it.
   f. Others see the vision and shares it to get others to pursue it with them.

Slide 6 of 100

3. Change your expectations to change your attitude.
   a. Attitude is your predisposition to life.
   b. Can be defined/described as a habit.
   c. A predisposition/habit can be described as your character.

Slide 7 of 100

FOUR STEPS TO DEVELOP NEW ATTITUDE/HABIT

➤ Identify your problem.

➤ Identify right thinking that will change you.

➤ Relate/identify with positive people

➤ Develop/implement plan/thinking for positive attitude.

Slide 8 of 100

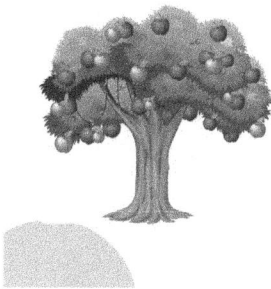

4. Change your attitude, change your <u>actions</u>.
   a. Your actions reflect your reputation.
   b. "Even a child is known by his deeds, whether he does what is pure and right" (Proverbs 20:11). Jesus said, "a tree is known by its own fruit" (Luke 6:44).

5. Change your actions, change your habits. Habits, "defines your position, i.e., your continual <u>thinking and actions</u>, i.e., "accomplished pianist."

5. Change your habits, change your character. First, we <u>think</u> it, we know it, we <u>dream</u> it, we focus on it, we <u>act</u> on it, that leads to <u>accomplishment</u>.

Lesson 2

Total Life Development

A. Introduction

1. Just as a person getting ready to run a marathon, they must make a mental and emotional decision to get physically fit for the event. So, the development of character means total life development.

2. Belief System Cycle:

Formation of Character:

Thinking/<u>Understanding</u> – Belief/<u>Conviction</u> – Expectations/<u>Vision</u> – Attitudes/<u>Values</u> – Actions/<u>Life</u> – Accomplishments/<u>Habits</u> – **CHARACTER**

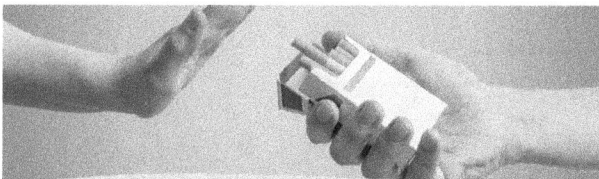

3. What is the most ridiculous argument for smoking that you have heard?
   a. It is all right to smoke because Rebekah "lighted off the camel" (Genesis 24:64).
   b. God approved smoking. "A smoking flax shall he not quench" (Isaiah 42:3).

B. Character Must Be Grounded on God's Plan

Believers must study the Bible to determine the principles by which they live.

1. How to discern biblical principles which develop character.

   a. Follow the clear <u>command</u> of Scriptures (Ephesians 6:1).

   b. Avoid a clear <u>negation</u> of Scriptures (Ephesians 4:31).

   c. Avoid circumstances that will <u>harm</u> your Christian life (1 Corinthians 6:14).

d. Be committed to a pure <u>through life</u> (Matthew 5:28).

e. Do not be a <u>stumbling</u> block for others (1 Corinthians 8:9).

f. Obey your <u>conscience</u>, do not violate it (James 4:17).

g. Do not intentionally harm your <u>body</u> (1 Corinthians 6:18-19).

h. Do not do anything that cannot be carried out in <u>faith</u> (Romans 14:23).

2. How to determine biblical principles.

   a. Must be trans <u>cultural</u> (Matthew 10:5).

   b. Must be trans <u>temporal</u> (Romans 13:1, 4).

   c. Look <u>beyond</u> the actual to the principle (Matthew 5:41).

C. Character Must Be Grounded On Thinking/Understanding

1. How to think about the Bible.

   a. Think with a <u>yielded</u> spirit.

   b. Ask the <u>Holy Spirit</u> to teach you (John 14:6).

   c. Think <u>practically</u>. Ask how you can apply this principle to your life.

   d. Think <u>holy</u>. Ask how you can become like God.

Slide 17 of 100

2. How to interpret the Bible.

   a. The golden rule of interpretation: "When the plain sense of Scriptures makes common sense, seek no other sense, but take every word at it's primary literal meaning." ~ David Cooper

   b. In light of the <u>historical context</u> – background.

   c. In light of the <u>author's original</u> plan and purpose.

   d. In light of the <u>context</u> (2 Peter 1:20).

   e. In light of the author's <u>meaning</u> of words.

Slide 18 of 100

D. Principles To Grow Character

1. The <u>Love</u> Principle. When properly motivated by love, you respect people and the law. You do right because you love others.

2. The <u>Loyalty</u> Principle. Because you have yielded to Christ, you do right to please Him.

3. The <u>Education</u> Principle. You do right because of what you have learned.

4. The <u>Training</u> Principle. You do right because you have done right so many times that it is a way of life with you.

Slide 19 of 100

5. The <u>Reward</u> Principle. You do right because of the satisfaction it gives.

6. The <u>Punishment</u> Principle. You do right because of the consequences you will get from doing wrong.

7. The <u>Fear</u> Principle. You do right because of unsettling emotions when you do wrong.

Slide 20 of 100

Lesson 3

Attitude Adjustments

Slide 21 of 100

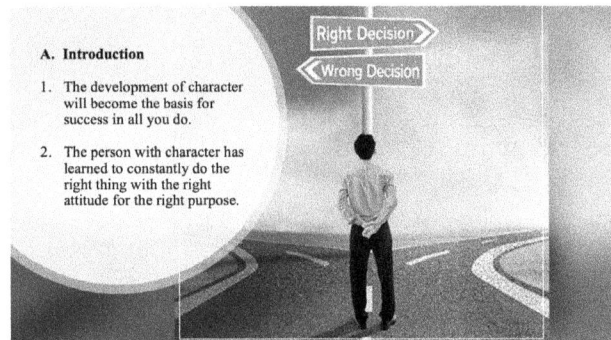

A. Introduction

1. The development of character will become the basis for success in all you do.

2. The person with character has learned to constantly do the right thing with the right attitude for the right purpose.

Slide 22 of 100

3. Belief System Cycle:

Formation of Character

Belief/<u>Conviction</u> – Expectations/<u>Vision</u> – Attitudes/<u>Values</u> – Actions/<u>Life</u> – Accomplishments/<u>Habits</u> – Thinking/<u>Understanding</u>
CHARACTER

Slide 23 of 100

4. Wrong attitudes lead to weak character.

   a. It's not my <u>responsibility</u>.

   b. No one will <u>see me</u> do it.

   c. No one <u>cares</u> if I do it.

   d. Everyone else is <u>doing it</u>.

Slide 24 of 100

B. Proper Attitudes Develop Character

1. Study influences. Who has greatly influenced you?

2. What makes a person successful in work? Carnegie Institute found 15% skills and 85% personality. Your personality is formed by attitudes and grows out of your character.

3. Why is a person fired? 30% incompetence, 53% personality, 27% other reasons.

Slide 25 of 100

4. You cannot determine your circumstances, but when you have the right attitude you get the best out of circumstances and rise above circumstances. Why me? Why this? Why now?

5. You cannot determine your emotional response, but when you have the right attitude, you can rise above your feelings. You cannot stop feelings, but you can keep your feelings from stopping you.

Slide 26 of 100

C. Bad Attitudes Will Keep You From Continuous Success

1. Wrong attitudes do five things to you.

   a. Sours your confidence.

   b. Misdirects your efforts.

   c. Dilutes your stamina and purpose.

   d. Jams your planning.

   e. Cuts you off from help.

Slide 27 of 100

2. If you think you are beaten, you are. If you think you dare not, you don't. If you would like to win, but think you cannot, it is almost certain you won't.

Slide 28 of 100

D. We Are Responsible For Our Attitudes

1. Don't give excuses.

   a. Marriage failed because married wrong.

   b. Job stagnate because don't like it.

   c. School goes bad because hate it.

2. Your lousy attitude is an option. You can change.

Slide 29 of 100

3. The pessimist complains about the wind. The optimist expects a better wind. The person with character changes the sail.

4. God tells you to take control of your attitude. "Constantly remind the people about these laws, and you yourself must think about them every day and every night so that you will be sure to obey all of them. For only then will you succeed. Yes, be bold and strong! Banish fear and doubt! For remember, the Lord your God is with you wherever you go." (Joshua 1:8-9, TLB).

Slide 30 of 100

5. Motivation to do good.

   a. Extrinsic – outward motivation

   b. Intrinsic – inward motivation

   c. Christocentric – "For me to live it Christ" (Philippians 1:21). Also see Philippines 4:13.

Slide 31 of 100

E. We Must Choose Good Attitudes

1. "Life is a choice." ~John Maxwell

2. God chooses what you will go thorough, you choose how you will go through it

Slide 32 of 100

3. "Every time you make a choice, you are turning the control part of you into something a little different from what it was before. And taking your life as a whole, with all its innumerable choices, you are slowly turning the control thing either into a heavenly creature or into a hellish one." ~C. S. Lewis

4. We can determine our strength of the following: faith, love, joy, peace, humility, kindness, and self-discipline.

Basis For Success In Christian Life And Service

A. Introduction

1. Development of biblical character is the basis for success in your Christian life and service.

2. What is Character?

   a. Webster: "Moral excellence and firmness."
   b. Oxford: "Moral constitution."
   c. Towns: "Moral character is your predisposition to right attitudes and right actions based on right reasons."
   d. The focus of your actions. The habit that guides your behavior. The controlling values of your personality.

3. What comes first, good character or good behavior?

4. Which of the following is based on biblical character?
   a. Doing right because I have never done wrong.
   b. Doing right because I am ignorant of wrong.
   c. Doing right because I am afraid I will get caught.
   d. Doing right because I will get rewards.
   e. Doing right because my friends do right.

5. The person with character has learned to consistently do the right thing with the right attitude for the right purpose.

B. The Belief System Cycle: Formation of Character

Belief/Conviction – Expectations/Vision – Attitudes/Values – Actions/Life –Accomplishments/Habits – Thinking/Understanding

CHARACTER

C. Comparison Of Right And Left Persons

1. The person with character has the ability to carry out a decision long after the emotions are gone that influenced the choice.

2. Left-sided people:
   a. Emotion based.
   b. What is easiest?
   c. When I feel good then I will do it.
   d. Controlled by moods.

   e. Selfish mind-set.
   f. Life and lips disagree.
   g. Looks for excuses.
   h. Outwardly influenced.
   i. Quits during tough times.
   j. This person whines.

3. Right-sided people:
   a. _Character_ based.
   b. What is _right_.
   c. When I do it, then I will _feel_ good.
   d. Controlled by _priorities_.
   e. _Servanthood_ mind-set.
   f. Life and lips _agree_.
   g. Looks for _solutions_.
   h. _Inwardly_ influenced.
   i. _Continue_ during tough times.
   j. This person _wins_.

4. "Right-sided people will have _long-lasting_ friendships, _successful_ marriages, _satisfying_ vocations, and an _inward_ happiness." ~John Maxwell

D. How To Step From The Left To The Right Side

1. Power of decisions. Make a _commitment_ to develop character (Luke 9:23).

2. Do right till the stars fall. Focus on _right reasons_ for all you do (Matthew 6:33).

3. You can do what you want to do. Establish a habit of doing things that are _right_ (Colossians 3:23).

4. Become _other person_ focused (Matthew 5:46).

5. Be firm in your commitment but be _patient and flexible_ with your inability to do all you desire (Jeremiah 1:6-7).

6. _Verbalize_ your principles so that you remember your expectations and how to apply them (Habakkuk 2:2).

7. _Track record_. When confronted with the problems and decisions of life:
   a. Look first to your _principles_.
   b. Gather all the _facts_ you can.
   c. Apply workable _solutions_ (Philippians 3:13-14).

8. Your success will give you confidence and build _character_ (Philippians 4:13).

Lesson 5

Dealing With Change And Growth

A. Introduction

1. Does character come naturally, or do you have to make changes to get character? When you grow, you change. When you grow in character, you make decisions based on what you know, and it affects your feelings. You cannot grow without change, but you can change without growth. Growth is _change toward a goal_.

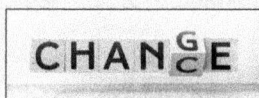

2. Observations of people with character:
   a. Everyone wants to change for the _better_.
   b. Everyone admires a person who had _changed for the better_.
   c. Very few people _change_ for the better.

Formation of Character

Thinking/Understanding – Belief/Conviction – Expectations/Vision – Attitudes/Values – Actions/Life – Accomplishments/Habits – **CHARACTER**

Slide 49 of 100

3. Wrong approaches to growth or change:
   a. You ask God to change a habit.
   b. You ask God to change your circumstances.
   c. You ask God to change people around you.
      RIGHT APPROACH: Ask God to change your approach to life.

Slide 50 of 100

4. Wrong things to change:
   a. You change your action without changing your thinking legalism.
   b. You change once without permanent adjustments experiments.
   c. You change outward without inward cosmetic.
   d. You keep changing your thinking confusion. You change your fruit without changing the root outward.

Slide 51 of 100

B. People With Character

1. Desire personal growth and development (Philippians 3:10).

2. Know how to grow and change (Philippians 3:13, 4:9), and have a strategy for growth and change.

3. Eliminate burdens and barriers (Hebrews 12:1).
   a. Negative. Get rid of distractions, weights, and hindrances.
   b. Positive. Become focused in your life.

Slide 52 of 100

4. Know how to overcome failure. Failure does not destroy you, your attitude toward failure stops you. We all have outward problems and disappointments within, but those with the will to win can overcome failure.
   a. There is a difference between "I failed" and "I am a failure." Don't war failure like a suit.
   b. Failure is part of the journey (1 Timothy 1:15).
   c. Don't let your failures control you.
   d. Learn something from every failure.
   e. Take responsibility, don't make excuses.

Slide 53 of 100

5. Have a dream/vision.
   a. Develop together. Does the person with vision go after character, or does the person with principles gravitate to purpose in life? What comes first?

   Character without vision examples.

   Vision without character productive.

   Both character and vision multiply effectiveness

Slide 54 of 100

   b. Live outside yourself. People with character live by principles outside themselves. People with vision are motivated to goals outside themselves.

   c. Applied action. When you have a vision, it moves you to actualize its potential. When vision grows out of character, the person sees exactly how to make it happen and has the power and principles to make it happen.

Slide 55 of 100

Lesson 6

Habits of the Heart

Slide 56 of 100

A. Introduction

1. The phrase, *Habits of the Heart*, was Tocqueville's description of America's virtue, character and morals.

2. Definition of habit: "A behavior pattern acquired by frequent repetition that is reflected in regular or increased performance."

3. Root: comes from root meaning clothing that is usually worn, i.e., a nun's habit.

4. No none is without habits, good and bad habits.

Slide 57 of 100

5. Habits are voluntary and involuntary.

6. Habits extend to every part of life:
   a. Language habits – thank you, cursing.
   b. Emotional habits – laughter, roll eyes.
   c. Physical habits – hand over cough, burp.
   d. Instinctive habits – drive car, stutter.

7. "If you do right, you will be right" Erin Towns, mother of Elmer Towns

Slide 58 of 100

B. How We Respond: A Habit Is A Way Of Responding That Has Been Learned

1. We think about the world:
   a. Remember. The ability to recreate the past and relate it to the present.
   b. Anticipate. The ability to predict a response or situation that will occur in the future.
   c. Imagine. The ability to conceive responses or situations that is not yet related to the present.

Slide 59 of 100

2. We perceive the world:

   a. To receive data. We can receive and understand information.

   b. To interpret data. We can give meaning to it and classify it with other information.

   c. To respond to data. We can respond properly to information. "The cat that sits on a hot stove, the cat will never sit on another hot stove, nor will the cat sit on a cold stove."

Slide 60 of 100

3. We fell about the world:

   a. Emotions are the response of your bodily state to a situation, anger, fear, alienation, depression.

   b. Feelings are the expression of the bodily state, happiness, strain, pressure, excitement.

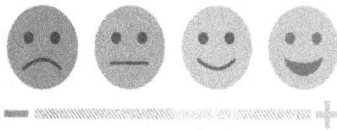

Slide 61 of 100

C. Do We Break Habits Or Make Habits?

1. A habit is formed by mere repetition: True or False

2. There is no such thing as a new habit, only the modification of old habits: True or False

3. Can we unlearn old habits by deliberate repetition to disintegrate the old? True or False

Slide 62 of 100

E. How To Break Old Habits

1. Know. Understand your situation and condition in life (Romans 7:18).

2. Look at self. Be aware of your actual weakness (Romans 7:19).

3. Evaluate. Measure the intensity of negative influence that your inadequacy contributes to your life (Romans 7:24).

Slide 63 of 100

4. Visualize. Form an image of ideal behavior that you desire (Romans 6:14).

5. Positionize. See the results will come to you for eliminating negative habits (Romans 8:2).

6. Want. Create and feel a desire to realize these ideals (Romans 6:11).

7. Reach. Look outside yourself for vision, strength, and help (1 Thessalonians 5:23).

Slide 64 of 100

8. Choice. Make a decision.

9. Act. Engage persistently in the desired response
   (1 Thessalonians 5:21).

10. Faith. Trust God to complete the action you have begun
    (1 Thessalonians 5:24).

Slide 65 of 100

Values And Morality

Slide 66 of 100

A. Introduction

1. The book, *Why Johnny Cannot Tell Right From Wrong* by William Kilpatrick, is a Catholic layman who attacks cultural relativism saying that nondirected methods of moral education which urges students to make equally valid choices in the jungle of relativism has actually encouraged youth to experiment with drug, sex, and lawlessness.

2. Values clarification is essentially doing what you want to or like to do, not what you ought to do.

Slide 67 of 100

B. Sources of Erosion in American Morality

1. Changing culture. Harvey Cox's book, *The Secular City* shows culture in six pictures:
   a. The tribe.
   b. The town.
   c. The metropolitan.
   d. The megalopolis.
   e. The switchboard, communication.
   f. The cloverleaf, transportation.

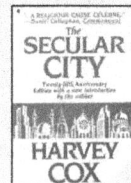

Slide 68 of 100

2. Conflicting values of new immigrants.

3. Public schools no longer a conduit of morality.

4. Making the Bible a myth rather than the source of morality.

5. Retreat of the church from effective teaching (*didache*) and preaching (the *Kerugma*).

Slide 69 of 100

C. Four Sources of Morality/Character: Suggested by David Reisman, *The Lonely Crowd*

1. Tradition-directed values. Represented by immigrants and transmitted through the family.
   a. Irish Catholic
   b. Scandinavian
   c. Oriental
   d. Hispanic
   e. African
   f. Others

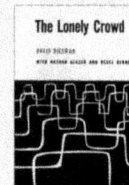

Slide 70 of 100

Actions/Habits – Attitudes/Values – Expectations/Aims –
Belief/Acceptance –Thinking/Why – CHARACTER

Slide 71 of 100

Authority: _____
Role Model: _____

Weakness:
  a. No outward biblical standard
  b. Conflict with traditional America
  c. Conflict with other ethnic groups because of no absolute standard.
  d. Not able to reproduce self when removed from its culture.
  e. Problems with differences in clothing, language, music, and other outward expressions.

Slide 72 of 100

104   HABITS OF THE HEART

2. Inner-Directed Values. Represented by traditional American values which are an amalgamation of biblical ethics, American "worth of the individual," and republicanism. These prizes: justice (do right), success (get ahead), and freedom (individualism).

Thinking/Understanding – Belief/Conviction – Expectations/Vision – Attitudes/Values – Actions/Life –Accomplishments/Habits – CHARACTER

Authority: _____

Role Model: _____

Weakness:
   a. Expect all to live by their values (superiority).
   b. Outward conformity produces legalism.
   c. Conflicts with the negative side of human nature.
   d. Openness and acceptance of other values becomes the seeds of its destruction.

3. Non-Driven Values (stimulus-response). Responds to or conforms to the pressures of others. Give in to the lower urges of the personality.
   a. Those who backslide from #1 or #2.
   b. Those who drop out of culture.
   c. A blend of the others.

Basic Drives/Lust – Stimulus Res./Want – Need/Fulfill/Good – Actions/Reinforced – Habits/Accomplishments – CHARACTER

Authority: _____

Role Model: _____

Weakness:
   a. Values are motivated by lower drives.
   b. Will not lift people beyond themselves.
   c. Ultimate needs are sacrificial to immediate needs.
   d. No basis to keep in check the negative side of the personality.
   e. Leads to destruction.
   f. No absolutes.

4. Autonomous-Directed Values. Expresses developing personality of the individual. This falls into two categories: the moral manager for efficiency and the moral therapist for self-actualization.

   a. The Moral Manager:
     1) Admires the self-made person.
     2) The motivation and strategy to attain is greater than the goal.

3) The standard to manage life comes from the marketplace.

4) Must manage resources and interpersonal relationship for calculated effectiveness.

5) Divide the expectations and activities of life into compartments of work, home, recreation, religions, etc. (dysfunctional).

6) The person is a sinner and takes control of their life.

b. The Moral Therapist:

1) Personal self-growth and actualization is the goal.

2) Accepts life's tensions arising from within the person and from the social, psychological and technological demands of society.

3) Life's focus is finding curses for growth and development.

4) Solutions take the form of enhancement or empowerment to meet outer demands and inner desires.

5) The standard for morality is a specialist who models resources for effective living or productivity.

6) Morality and character are the liberation, development, and fulfillment of individual.

Need/<u>Desire To Develop</u> – Focus/<u>Attain Self-Actualization</u> –
Organizes/Administers/<u>Resources</u> – Controlled/<u>Action</u> –
Receives/<u>Worth</u> – CHARACTER

Authority: _____
Role Model: _____

Weakness:
    a. No absolutes in basis for morality.
    b. Man is the center of morality.
    c. No solutions with conflicting cultures and systems.
    d. Must oppose biblical morality to validate its existence.

D. How To Develop Character In A Hostile Culture

Thinking/Understanding:
1. Know <u>God</u>, who is the source of your morals.
2. Know the <u>reasons</u>, proof and how to apply your principles.

Beliefs/Assurance:
3. Make a total <u>commitment</u> to the demands of Scriptures.
4. Yield body, soul, and mind to Jesus Christ.

Expectations/Vision:
5. Realize God will give you <u>power</u> to overcome all things.
6. Identify with those who will reinforce your biblical aspirations.

Values/Attitudes:
7. Identify the <u>principles</u> by which you live.
8. Challenge all negative values that creep into your life. Don't
    feed them and reject their presupposition.

Actions/Life:
9. Recognize the power that flows from right decision.
10. Do not wait for good feeling to do right, do right and you will
    <u>feel good</u>.

Accomplishments/Habits:
11. If you do <u>right</u>, you will be <u>right</u> (character).

Lesson 8

Breaking The Bondage

A. Introduction

Some people are in bondage to
habits they cannot break. They
have tried unsuccessfully to free
themselves but have failed. Their
problem is not a physical or mental
one. They have a *besetting sin* that
keeps them in bondage (Hebrews
12:1). This lesson gives steps to
breaking the bondage of habits.

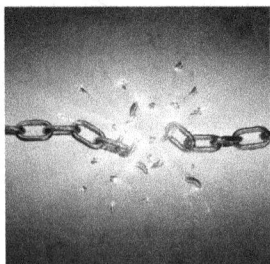

1. <u>Head knowledge</u>. You know God is all powerful.

2. <u>Helpless victim</u>. You cannot break the power of your nature,
    satan, habits, etc.

3. <u>Problem is lies</u>. Satan's power is in lying to you. "You are of
    your father the devil, and the desires of your father you want to
    do . . . for he is a liar" (John 8:44).

4. Center of control. Your mind controls your life. Whatever controls your mind has power over you. "For the weapons of our warfare are not carnal but mighty in God . . . casting down arguments and every high thing that exalts itself against the knowledge of God, bringing every thought into captivity to the obedience of Christ" (1 Corinthians 10:4-5).

A. Six Steps To Breaking The Cycle Of Habits That Have You In Bondage

1. You must recognize and renounce any control over your mind that is not Christ. "As the serpent deceived Eve by his craftiness, so your minds may be corrupted from the simplicity that is in Christ" (1 Corinthians 11:3).

a. Anti-Christian or ungodly home, godless influence, alien bond.

b. Were you involved innocently or actively in an occult, new age, spiritism, black or white magic, cults, or other religions?

c. Satanic rituals.

d. Pray, "I recognize…"

2. You must acknowledge any self-deception and embrace the truth of God.
   a. Recognizing freedom begins with the mind (Psalm 51:6).
   b. Recognize self-deception in: Hearing but not doing Scriptures, "deceiving your own selves" (James 1:22). Not admitting your sin, "We deceive ourselves" (1 John 1:8). Thinking we are something, "thinks himself" (Galatians 6:3). Thinking we are smart, "deceive himself" (1 Corinthians 3:18). By sinning, "be not deceived" (1 Corinthians 6:9).
   c. Pray, "I admit …"

3. You must forgive others to overcome bitterness and get freedom.

   a. If you refuse to forgive, satan has an advantage over you (2 Corinthians 2:10-11).

   b. Make a list of their names, not their sins.

   c. When you continually bring up the past, you have not forgiven them.

   d. Forgiveness is a choice. Since God requires you to forgive, it is something you can you.

e. You naturally want revenge because you suffered.

f. When you don't want to let them off the hook, it means they still have their hooks in you. You are in bondage to them.

g. You don't forgive them for their sake, you forgive them for your sake.

h. The issue is no longer between you and them, but between you and God.

i. When you forgive, you choose to live with their consequences. If you do not forgive, you still live with bitter consequences.

j. You can choose whether to live in the freedom of forgiveness or the bitterness of bondage.

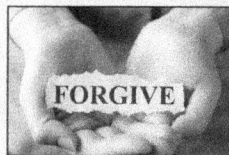

k. Pray, "I forgive…"

FORGIVE

4. You must overcome rebellion in your life by submitting to the authority of God and those over you.

   a. Being under authority is an act of faith. You trust God and His line of authority to lead your life.

   b. We are to submit to: civil government (Romans 13:1-7); church leadership (Hebrews 13:17), parents (Ephesians 6:1-3); husband (1 Peter 3:1-4), employers (1 Peter 2:13-23); God (Daniel 9:5, 9).

   c. Pray, "I submit…"

5. You must overcome <u>bondage</u> in your life through the freedom of Jesus Christ.

   a. To sin habitually without self-control is to be in <u>bondage</u>.

   b. Jesus Christ wants you to be free (John 8:36), but what about your sins and failures?

   c. Freedom is not being passive. You are free to do (active) what you want to do. The key is to take responsibility for your actions. You get two virtues when you confess, <u>cleansing and forgiveness</u> (1 John 1:9).

Slide 97 of 100

   d. How many times can you get forgiveness? Many people suffer the "confession box" cycle of Roman Catholics. They go back to sin after confession because they are in bondage.

   e. Don't just say, "I am sorry for it" but say, "I am <u>responsible</u> for it." Our responsibility is to not allow sin to habitually control our bodies (Romans 6:13).

   f. <u>Renounce</u> every sin done to your body by you or another.

   g. Pray, "I take responsibility…"

Slide 98 of 100

6. You must renounce sinful influences that come by family and acquaintances.
   a. You are <u>predisposed</u> by several sources:
      1) Inward despair.
      2) Genetically.
      3) Immoral atmosphere.
      4) Wrong heroes.
      5) Direct sinful stimulation.
      6) Satanic/demonic activity.

Slide 99 of 100

   b. <u>Disown</u> the sins of others and their influences on your life Galatians 5:24; Exodus 20:4-5).

   c. <u>Recognize</u> you have been crucified, buried and raised with Jesus Christ and you now sit in the heavenlies (2 Corinthians 4:14).

   d. <u>Publicly</u> state you belong to the Lord Jesus Christ (Galatians 5:24).

   e. <u>Verbally</u> claim the blood of Jesus over the evil one (1 Corinthians 6:20; 1 John 1:7).

   f. Pray, "I renounce…"

Slide 100 of 100

PART FOUR

HABITS OF THE HEART

ADDITIONAL RESOURCES

POWERPOINT SLIDES:

To purchase and download the Powerpoint Slides go to
https://www.norimediagroup.com/pages/elmer-towns

VIDEO:

To purchase available video by Dr Towns go to
https://www.norimediagroup.com/pages/elmer-towns

ADD-ON CONTENT

To purchase additional products in this series go to
https://www.norimediagroup.com/pages/elmer-towns

RELATED BOOKS

Available at https://www.norimediagroup.com/pages/elmer-towns